WITH SA'DI IN THE GARDEN

WITH SA'DI IN THE GARDEN

OR

THE BOOK OF LOVE

BEING

THE "ISHK" OR THIRD CHAPTER OF THE "BOSTAN"

OF THE PERSIAN POET SA'DI

EMBODIED IN A DIALOGUE HELD IN THE GARDEN OF THE

TAJ MAHAL, AT AGRA

SIR EDWIN ARNOLD, M. A., K. C. I. E., C. S.I.

GYAN

Published by

GYAN

Gyan Publishing House
5, Ansari Road
Daryaganj, New Delhi-110002
Phone: 011-47034999, 9811692060
E-mail: books@gyanbooks.com

Distribution Network
gyanbooks.com
India, USA, Canada, UK, Australia, France

ISBN : 978-81-212-9236-8 (PB)
First Published, 1888

2nd Impression 2023

Printed at: Gyan Press, Delhi.

WITH SA'DI IN THE GARDEN
Author: SIR EDWIN ARNOLD

WITH SA'DI IN THE GARDEN

OR

THE BOOK OF LOVE

WITH SA'DI IN THE GARDEN

OR

The Book of Love

BEING

THE "ISHK" OR THIRD CHAPTER OF THE "BOSTAN" OF THE PERSIAN POET SA'DI

Embodied in a Dialogue held in the Garden of the Taj Mahal, at Agra

BY

SIR EDWIN ARNOLD, M.A., K.C.I.E., C.S.I.

AUTHOR OF "THE LIGHT OF ASIA," ETC., ETC.

BOSTON
ROBERTS BROTHERS
1888

This Volume is Dedicated

TO

THE RIGHT HON. THE EARL OF DUFFERIN, K.P.

ETC., ETC., ETC.

Viceroy and Governor-General of India,

WITH

THE AUTHOR'S RESPECT, ADMIRATION, AND ATTACHMENT.

[NOTE.—The sections in this poem taken directly from the Persian are printed in italics, and present the third chapter of the Bôstân nearly as it stands in the text of Sa'di. The bulk of the poem is original, though some passages imitate the Persian manner. Utmost acknowledgments are due to the prose translation of "The Bôstân," by Capt. H. Wilberforce Clarke, R. E., one of the very best and most faithful ever made from an Oriental classic. Those familiar with Persian literature will be aware of certain necessary modifications. The accomplished singing-girls are types from the life.]

PROEME.

Sweet Friends! who love the Music of the Sun,
And listened — glad and gracious — many an one,
While, on a light-strung lyre, I sought to tell
Indian Siddartha's wisdom; and the spell
Of Jayadev's deep verse; and proud deeds wrought
By Pandu Princes; and how gems are fraught
With meanings; and to count each golden bead
Of Allah's names of Beauty; and to read
High tender lessons Upanîshads teach —
"Secret of Death," and subtle soul of speech
In holy OM; and to con — line by line —
The lofty glory of the "Lay Divine" —
Arjuna's speech with Krishna: — once more come,
And listen to the Vina and the Drum!
Come once more with me from our sombre skies
To hear great Sa'di's tuneful mysteries —
"Nightingale of a thousand lays" — for he
Will, 'mid the Garden, sing in many a key

Rare Persian airs. But, tell them first, my Song!—
Lest they do thee, and me, and Sa'di wrong—
To come with hearts to gentle thoughts inclined,
Since this is only for the wise and kind;
And, of itself, our Garden shuts its gate
On him that's hard, cold, uncompassionate;
But opens wide its alleys, green and still,
To Sesame of Love and fair Good-will!

Schooner Yacht "Hadassah," off Portland;
July 12, 1888.

WITH SA'DI IN THE GARDEN;

OR,

THE BOOK OF LOVE.

Introduction.

At Agra we had seen the City-sights,
The Fort, the Mosques, the busy hot bazaars;
Akbar's red bulwarks, — shutting treasures in
With league-long ramp of sandstone, — Hathi Pul,
The Bathing-House of Mirrors, Ghuznee's Gates,
Diwan-i-Khas, Diwan-i-Am, the Court
Of Jasmine, Machi Bhawun, and that gem
Of holy places named the "House of Pearl" —
Motî-Musjid, where Archangels might pray
And miss no grace of Heaven, no purity! —
Under the zigzagged cream and rosy roof
Of Jâhânâra's Mosque our unshod feet

Had lingered, mid the Muslim worshippers;
To Itimad-ud-Dowlah's sepulchre —
By will of Nourmahal, "Light of the world,"
Upreared and carved — we had made pilgrimage;
And, at Sikandra, to great Akbar's tomb;
And once, and twice, and thrice, to Taj-Mahal.

Ah, the white wonder! Have there been who came
And gazed, — and laid staff and surveying chain
Along thy sacred sides, Fairest of fanes!
To turn away, saying, "The plan errs thus!
The plinth lacks this! the arch was ill-conceived!
'T is but a cube of stone with angles lopped!
Much seems yet needed to the architraves!
The lattice gives no light! the casing-stones
Are mere veneer?" Measurers parcel-blind
Who, with yard-rule would count the inches off
From Aphrodite's Parian majesty,
And stretch tape o'er Elysian asphodel!

He hath not eyes to see whose eyes have seen
That glory of the beauty of the Taj,
Nor knew and felt — at seeing — how man's hand
Comes nearest God's herein, touching His charm
Of rounded silvery clouds in that poised Dome
Which hangs between the sky's blue and the stream's —
Fixing the fleeting structures of His snow
In those piled pilasters and stainless flats
Which mount and mount — delicate, drifted, still; —
Simple, yet subtle, as the curves and shades
Of the white breasts of her it celebrates,
Arjamand Banu, Queen of Love and Death:
A passion, and a worship, and a faith
Writ fast in alabaster, so that Earth
Hath nothing anywhere of mortal toil
So fine-wrought, so consummate, so supreme —
So, beyond praise, Love's loveliest monument —
As what in Agra, upon Jumna's bank,
Shah Jahan builded for his Lady's grave.

Oh, friends! verse is too bold seeking to tell
How beautiful this Eastern Tomb doth rise,
How fair by sun or moonlight, how superb
This house of Love and Death — all lily-white
In the green garden upon Jumna's shore!
The City, swarming past the River's bend,
Wafts no noise here; far off you may discern
The bridge of boats, the Fort's red wall, the Domes —
Three pearly foam-bells — of the Mosque of Pearl
Suspended o'er those distant parapets;
Ram-Bagh; the tall palm-groves by Akbar's grave;
And Akbar's judgment-terrace. Here the stream —
Yamuna, silver daughter of the Sun —
Glides broad and silent, washing sandy flats
And ancient water-gates. By avenues
Of neem and palsa; past low huts of mat,
Gay painted country-dwellings, topes, and wells,
Temples, and little shrines where gilded gods
Squat with crossed legs — Balkrishna, Hanuman;

By pân and bangle shops, by weaving-grounds,
By creaking Persian wheels, rice-fields, and tanks
Winds the cantonment-way, made populous
With tread of patient feet, which come and go
Doing the errands of their placid day.
You meet the brown-limbed laden coolie girls,
The ekkas with full freight of pots and wives,
The camels stalking slow, the palanquins,
The belted peon, the sweetmeat-man, the ox
Grave-pacing with his spurting water-skins;
The spangled dancing-girls, the fishermen,
Byrâgis, sepoys, hamals, jungle-folk,
The people of an Agra afternoon:
When, suddenly, — wheels stop, bridles are drawn,
One cries, "The Taj!" We are at entrance gate
Of India's pride, the Tomb, the House of Rest
For Mumtaz-i-Mahal, the "Exalted one" —
Queen of her Sultan's heart, and Hindostan —
Here by her Lord and Lover laid to sleep.

And here, too, sleeps the stately King who planned
This splendor for his sorrow — Shah Jahan —
Twelve score years back Sultan of India,
Ruler august, and sire of Aurangzebe.

First a proud archway, reared of rosy stone
Banded with marble; and a frontal wall
Crowned by low cupolas. The demi-vault
Of entry towers aloft, framing huge space
Of azure heaven, broad-groined with span and rib
In marbles brown and white; and, all the bands,
String-courses, cornices, range thick-inlaid
With scriptures from the Holy Book, tall scrolls
Writ in commanding Toghra — Alif, Lam,
Ghain, and their solemn sister characters,
Marching with step severe, and measured sweep,
Mim, Nun, and Waw and Sin, made ornaments
To deck the door, and issue doctrines true:
"*No God save God! In name of God the One!*"

Along the spandrels; on the coping-stones
Tender deep things from Sura sixty-seven —
The "Chapter of the Kingdom" — blazoning
"*Blessed is He that hath the Kingdom! He*
Made Life and Death to prove ye; and He made
The seven spheres of Heaven — each by each;
Say he is God the Merciful!" and, then,
"*Only the pure of heart enter the gates,*
Enter God's Garden!"

See! that might be this,
If Paradise had portals like Jahan's!
For, through the vaulted door, opens to sight
A glorious garden — green, forever green,
Since hither comes no harsh nor biting time
To strip the buds, but, all the warm year through,
The palms rise feathered, and the pipal-boughs
Whisper men's doings to the listening gods
With watchful leaves; citrons and rose-apples

Keep their bright blossoms and their jewelled fruits,
And broad bananas flaunt their silken flags.
The spacious Pleasaunce shows on either hand
Dark verdant banks of various foliage —
Cooling the eyes, and quieting the heart —
With parterres interspersed, and rose-thickets,
And sheets of fiery Indian marigolds,
Moon-flowers, and shell-flowers ; crimson panoply
Of the silk-cottons, and soft lilac light
Where sunbeams sift through Bougainvilliers :
Pink oleander-sprays you mark, fig-blooms,
Stars of the champak, tulip-cups, and spikes
Of silver-studded aloes, with red gold
Of peacock-bushes, and fair deadly bells
Of white datura. What most holds the eye,
Leading it onward towards the sight of sights,
Is yon black avenue of thuja-trees
With cypress intermixed, ranged, all the way,
On either border of the broad paved path,

Like sentinels of honor. From the gate
Straight to the threshold of the Taj-Mahal
Those trees of mourning marshal you! Between
Gleams the paved way, laid smooth in slabs of white
River-like running through the banks of green;
And, on this middle pavement — all its length —
Wan water lies entanked, its crystal face
Rippled with gliding fish, and lotus-leaves
By the wind rocked, and rain of fountain-drops;
For — all its length — jets of thin silver dart
Into the Blue, and sparkle back to the Blue
Reflected in those marble-margined pools.
Led thus by sombre cypresses, and lines
Of dancing water-jets, and lilied tanks,
And glistering garden-causeway, the gaze lights
On that great Tomb, rising prodigious, still,
Matchless, perfect in form, a miracle
Of grace, and tenderness, and symmetry,
Pearl-pure against the sapphire of the sky!

Enchanted, the foot follows the fixed gaze,
Which marks no more the garden's wealth, the
pools,
The tall, dark sentry-trees, the shining path,
The enlaced and rustling bamboos, the plumed palms
With doves and sun-birds in their swinging crowns;
Only it dwells on that strange shape of grace
Instinct with loveliness — not masonry!
Not architecture! as all others are,
But the proud passion of an Emperor's love
Wrought into living stone, which gleams and soars
With body of beauty shrining soul and thought,
Insomuch that it haps as when some face
Divinely fair unveils before our eyes —
Some woman beautiful unspeakably —
And the blood quickens, and the spirit leaps,
And will to worship bends the half-yielded knees,
While breath forgets to breathe: so is the Taj;
You see it with the heart, before the eyes

Have scope to gaze. All white! snow-white! cloud-
white!
Like a white rounded cloud seems that smooth dome
Seated so stately mid its sister-domes,
Waxing to waist, and waning to wan brow;
White, too, the minarets, like ivory towers,—
Four tall Court ladies tending their Princess—
Set at the four shorn corners. Near and far
The garden clasps the Sanctuary in folds
Of rounded verdure; on its right and left
Rise two fair Musjids, Chapels of the shrine,
Themselves in other spot majestical:
The one which looks to Mecca is for prayer,
This other, the Juwáb—for-symmetry—
Offers a resting-house where men may sit
And hear the Bulbul singing to the Rose,
And talk of Arjamand, and Love and Death.
Behind the glorious Tomb a court, a wall,
A bank which drops to Jumna, and, beyond—

Over the River, where her Emperor died —
Brindâban, and a hundred leagues of plain.

Hushed, you advance — your gaze still fixed! heart, soul
Full of the Wonder; drinking in its spell
Of purity and mystery, its poise
Magical, weird, aerial; the ghost
Of Thought draped white — as if that Sultan's sigh
Had lived in issuing from his love and grief
Immense, and taken huge embodiment
Which one rash word might change from Tomb to Cloud.
But mount the first great platform — sandstone, red,
A thousand feet each way — and, coming nigh,
You shall perceive the sovereignty of this
Which utmost loveliness did somewhile hide.
Now grows the mighty greatness of the Taj
Plainer! 't is eighty feet of marble snow

From the embroidered fillet of yon Dome
To its gold Crownal, glittering in the sky
A hundred "yards of Akbar" from the ground.
Under that Saracenic entry-arch
These palms might grow, nor brush a topmost plume
Against the key-stone. Hence, too, shall you see
As if the Empress' self drew near, and near,
Till her blue veins showed, and her brows, and gems,
How opulent the unsullied marble spreads
With ornament, how decked with precious work
Of scroll and spray, volute and chasery,
And grave texts written clear in black and red
Inlaid upon the white; not marring it
More than those blue veins mar a lady's neck;
More than her pencillings of lash and brow
Break totalness of spotless skin and limb.

Mount, now, this second stair, arriving so
On upper platform, paved with marble pale,

Each way three hundred feet. Here stands the
Taj!
This is the snowy table-land wherefrom
Rises the House of snow, mountainous, pure,
As any topmost peak of Himalay!
A massy square; the angles shorn; each face
Pierced with a vaulted entrance, parted off
From too keen worship of the Sun — who loves
Arjamand's bed — from too direct a ray
Of Indian moonlight, by those panelled doors
Of lace-cut alabaster. Nearer draw
And note their wondrous toil — the white rock wrought
To exquisite, entangled, tracery
Intricate-patterned; knit, like midnight dreams
Of some geometer, in governed curves
Cissoid, parabola, and lemniscate,
Rhombus, and rhomboid, cirque, trapezium,
Each absolute, if eye shall follow them;
Strong as cast steel, but delicate as veil

Of filmy web from Dacca's patient loom
Ten folds whereof left Akbar's daughter bare,
So that the Mogul cried: "Com'st thou unclad?"
Thus, by a hundred marble lattices
Passes the daylight to their place of rest,
Shorn of its glare; but you — before you pass —
Note, too, this diaper-work of branch and leaf
On door-post, lintel, and long cornices;
And how the black embroidering lines and texts,
Strict-marshalled from the Arab alphabet,
Serve the broad beauty of the pearly walls
For softening shadows, how the Finial —
Pointing with gold the moon-round cupola —
Crowns with thin crescent its fair-lifted swell;
How — near approached — faint stains and wandering veins
Show on the marble — azure, saffron, rose —
So that it hath not coldness, like to snow,
But in large purity takes, glad, the sun,

And answers him with tender tint and glow,
As if the milky marble lived, indeed.

You enter, reverent: — for a Queen is here,
And the dead King who loved her; and Death's self
Who ends all — and begins all; and Love's might
Which greater is than Death, and heeds him not.
White! white! tenderly, softly, white — around,
Above, beneath — save that the praying floor
Is laid in dark squares, and the architrave
Runs comely with adornings staid, and script
Of Toghra text. See! read! "*His Majesty,*
Shadow of God, Mûjtahid of the age,
Built this for Resting-Place of Arjamand."
And, elsewhere: — "*Jesus said, (on Whom be peace!)*
This world a Bridge is; pass thou over it,
But build no House of Hope there." And, again,
The Fatihah — "*In the name of God most High*
The Clement, the Compassionate!" Four tombs

Of Princes and Princesses — kindred bones —
Surround the shrine; here, in the heart of all,
With chapels girdled, shut apart by screens,
The shrine's self stands. White, delicately white!
White as the cheek of Mumtaz-i-Mahal
When Shah Jahan let fall a king's tear there, —
White as the breast her new babe vainly pressed
That ill day in the camp at Burhanpur,
The fair shrine stands, guarding two Cenotaphs:
For, when the Trumpet of Serâfil blows,
They shall not rise herefrom; their happy dust
Sleeps in one earth beneath, where two plain stones,
Hers in the midst, and his — raised half a span
(For lordliness of sex and Empery)
But close beside it — mark their very graves.
This is but record of them, two Death-Chests
O'er-flowered upon white marble with bright sprays
And colored buds and blooms, posies of Death

Softly enamelled: on the Emperor's bier
The Kalamdàn, noting a Mussulman
Dead in the Faith; on hers verses in black
Praising the name of Allah, and her name,
And when she lived and died — of all that time
The Glory, and the Cynosure, and Pearl.

All which rare work is over-canopied
With vaulted inner roof of milk-white blocks
Contracting, tier by tier, — till, far above,
A cap-stone shuts the canopy, so high
Those letters of the "Throne verse" cubit-long
Show like the little writing on a gem.
And, ever, in the womb of that white roof,
Echoes sigh round and round, low murmurings,
Voices aerial, by a word evoked —
A foot-fall. Yet it will not render back
Ill noises, or a rude and scurrile sound:
But if some woman's lips and gentle breath

Utter a strain, if some soft bar be played,
Some verse of hymn, or Indian love-lament,
Or chord of Seventh, the white walls listen close,
And take that music, and say note for note
Softly again ; and then — echoing themselves —
Reverberate their melting antiphones,
Low waves of harmony encountering waves
And rippling on the rounded milky shores,
And making wavelets of new harmonies.
Thus — fainter, fainter — higher, higher — sighing
The music dieth upwards ; but so sweet,
So fine and far, and lingering at the last,
You cannot tell when Silence comes : the air,
Peopled by hovering Angels, still seems full
With stir celestial, with foldings down
Of pinions ; and those heavenly parting notes
As tender, as if great Isrâfil's self —
Who hath the sweetest voice in all God's worlds —
Still whispered o'er the tomb of Arjamand !

The milk-white marvel of this inner shrine
Is carved in Jâli-work of tracery —
One panel of the tracery a slab
Five cubits every way, fretted and pierced
To marble gauze — so that the sunbeams, dimmed,
Steal, like gold twilight, to their mighty names
And show them well-nigh as if whispering them.
But yet a greater wonder! for its sides —
Where the smooth stone spreads whole — holds inlaid
wealth
Of fair delicious fancies, wreath and sprig,
Blown tulip, and closed rose, lilies and vines,
All done in cunning finished jewellery
Of precious gems — jasper and lazulite,
Sardonyx, onyx, blood-stone, golden-stone,
Carnelian, jade, crystal, and chalcedony,
Turkis, and agate; and the berries and fruits
Heightened with coral-points and nacre-lights
(One single spray set here with five-score stones)

So that this place of death is made a bower
With beauteous grace of blossoms overspread;
And she who loved her garden, lieth now
Lapped in a garden.

And all this for Love!

The marbles were Mukrâni — Jeypore's best —
Brought seventy koss in creaking cattle-wains;
The sandstone Futtehpur's; the jewels came
Over a hundred wastes, a thousand hills,
By camel-caravan, ten thousand bales,
From Balkh, Iran, and far-off Khorasàn.
Three crores our Emperor lavished on his Taj;
Two lakhs of workmen toiled for seventeen years
Accomplishing the Death-Place of his Queen:
And, all for Love! Dying at Burhanpur
She spake to him: "Oh, Sultan of the Age!
Life of my Soul! who lov'dst me so; and knowest
How well I loved! now pass I — leaving thee
Last babe and latest kiss. Let all the world

Know thy great love and mine; and build for me
For Mumtaz dead — thy Persian wife — a Tomb
Which Earth shall marvel at, and all men laud,
Extolling thee, and not forgetting me."
And Jahan cried: "Yea! but by God the Truth!
This thing shall be; the world shall know of thee;
Thou shalt have such a tomb!" Whereon she died
In child-bed — after fifteen wedded years —
And Shah Jahan builded the Taj Mahal.

I have two pictures of Queen Arjamand
In the Persian manner. Oh, a lady fair!
Everywhere beautiful, and born for love;
A face to win worship of hearts, once seen.
No vain voluptuous Odalisque, with orbs
Set bold under low brow, but kind, but good,
More woman than Sultana; yet with air
Of majesty, as fitted great Princess;
And in her high-bred nostrils, habit of rule.

Complexion like the shell of ostrich-egg,
A tinted ivory; hair midnight black,
Braided in seven bright tresses; dark brown eyes
Splendidly lambent under eyebrows arched
Like edge of swallow's wing; — love-lighted eyes
Curtained with long, fine, sweeping eyelashes;
Cheeks hardly touched by palest rose-color;
Chin delicately moulded; sweetest mouth
Flower-soft and sensitive, with curves to make
The smile divine — a mouth of rose and pearl —
Mouth to give orders to an Emperor:
The neck an alabaster pillar; hands
Perfect and small; but stained upon the palms
With henna's russet-red, the Persian way,
Holding a blossom of the pomegranate
Flower of true Faith! Upon the proud smooth head
A Persian cap of state sewn thick with pearls;
Necklet and ear-rings pearl; a ruby clasps
The scarlet silken choli laced with gold

Binding her high-girt breasts ; a shawl of blue
Sits on her comely shoulders, stiff with gold,
Letting a dagger's jewelled handle peer ;
And cloth of gold, clasping a slender waist,
Droops to the feet, slippered in silver, gemmed.
Arjamand Banu Begam — such she was.

Why tell all this ? That you may know the Queen
They buried ; and the beauteous burying-place
Where, that last day at Agra, certain ones
Sate in the left-hand Mosque, surnamed Juwâb
And heard, in shadow of her sepulchre,
Sa'di's deep Chapter touching Love and Death.
For said the Munshi, "'T is full moon to-night !
What if you once more view the Taj thereby ?" —
Good Mirza Hussein he, Muslim — and more —
Sûfi, far seen in deep philosophies,
Who knew grave secrets hid in subtle verse
Of Hafiz — underneath that merry veil

Of "Taverns," "Wine-cups," and the "Magian Boy"—
Knew Ishk, and teachings of Tusawwuf, knew
Hakîkat, Tariyat—as darkly shows
Gulshan-i-Raz, the "Mystic Rose Garden;"
A wise, and well-esteemed, and courteous Sage;
And he, the Saheb—my life-long friend—replied
Smilingly: "Excellent! if you would read
Sa'di's third chapter of the Bostân there
That 'Ishk' which sings of Love—you who can make
The Persian plain to us; since, good it were
To hear the tender couplets Mumtaz heard
There, in her Pleasaunce, by her Sepulchre;
And speak of Love, and what it is, and how,
And whither it should lead us, and God's will
Fashioning Beauty so to seize and sway
By grace so great; and these strange hearts of men
To passion for it, even to folly and death,
To mourn it with such splendor sorrowful
As yon white lordly anguish of the Taj.

Bring the scrolls, Mirza! and the reading-stool,
And Gulbadan, that Delhi girl, who sings
Ghazals so well, and Dilazâr, her mate,
Who plays bandoora, and knows dance and song.
Ask them to come; say there'll be fruits and cakes
With golden mohurs; and meet me at the gate.
The Taj shall be Shirâz, and we will sit
In its green garden, underneath the moon,
To read the 'Ishk' and hear the nightingales
Make music to the Rose in our Bostân."

"Inshallạh!" Mirza Hussein said: "Please God!
This will be so. Sa'di hath much to teach,
And Gulbadan shall bring her waiting-girl
With lamps and bells, and summon Dilazâr.
At nightfall we will come."

Thus it befell
Those five were gathered at the Mosque Juwâb

By dusk: — the Mirza; gentle Gulbadan
The Persian singer, with the melting voice;
Dark Dilazâr, handsome, and bold, and skilled
To play for every song and step; the maid
Attending them; and last, that Englishman,
That Saheb I knew, lover of India.
Too much her lover! for his heart lived there
How far soever wandered thence his feet.
Some said — amongst the Buddhists — he had dwelled
Of old in Indian towns, and was re-born
In cold, hard, unbelieving Frangestan
Outcast, for ancient faults to expiate;
Some, that in days of the great mutiny,
The dark Mahratta maidens laid the spell
Of love and hidden teachings on his soul;
Some that he dreamed the West and East would meet
On some far day, by some fresh-opened path,
In sisterly new Truths, and strove for that:
I think he did but find Wisdom's wide stream

Nearest the fountain clearest, India's air
Softer and warmer than his native skies;
And liked the gentle speech, the grave reserve,
The piety and quiet of the land,
Its old-world manners, and its reverent ways,
And kind simplicity of Indian homes,
And classic comeliness of Indian girls
More than his proper people, and his tasks.
He was to blame, but he loved India.

In the Garden of the Taj.

"SPREAD, Khadim!" quoth the Mirza "by this wall
The mats and cushions; trim the copper lamp,
Set forth the fruit and cakes where Gulbadan
May keep her lips from too much idleness;
Bring Dilazâr's tamboora! see no snake
Hath crept among the carpets; *âg lejao!*
To light the kallians for the Saheb and me:
And let none trouble us!" The garden-guard
Obeyed with "*Achcha! achcha!*" tied our gift
Into the corner of his cloth; salaamed,
And left us to the mosque-floor, and the scroll,
The tomb, the still trees, and the Indian night.

SAHEB. Now, Gulbadan! — while Mirza Hussein seeks
His starting-place in this old Persian book
Where our dead Poet keeps melodious grave —
Sing some light strain to tell the nightingales
We and the Roses watch! Dilazâr's hand
Has strung tamboora's strings to key of C —
Three wires of steel and one of brass, all stretched
Ready for every lovely lay you know —
We will begin with music.

GULBADAN. Will this please
The ear, I wonder, of my English lord?
Dilazâr knows the ghazal, and it seems
Made for our garden, named "*Shirîn, Shirîn.*"

Therewith she stooped, to touch, upon her feet
The peal of silver bells which tinkled there;
Murmuring the little prayer that singing girls
Make, before lifting voice or fingering string,

To Pîr, or Guardian-Saint:—such pious ways
Have these whom many scorn! And then she sang:

[GULBADAN *sings.*]

A Lover said: "For one touch of her hand
I would give Balkh, I would give Samarkand,
So sweet she is!" the Bulbul sang between
"Rose of rare sweetnesses! *Shirîn, Shirîn!*"

The Sultan heard: "By Allah! this is much!
Two cities which my sword gained, for one touch!
How rich he seems!" The Bulbul sang between
"Rose of rich sweetnesses! *Shirîn, shirîn!*"

The Lover said: "When I may kiss her feet
I am so happy that all life grows sweet."
The Sultan mused: the Bulbul sang between
"Rose of blown happiness! *Shirîn, Shirîn!*"

"Oh! Rose" the Sultan said, "but, hast thou heard
This Lover's boasting, and thine answering bird?"

The Rose blushed while she sighed: "It is well seen!
Love is enough! *Shirîn, shirîntarîn!*"

"Oh, Sultan!" said the Nightingale, "I die
Pierced by the thorn, yet, glad at heart am I!
Sweet, ever sweeter, sweetest, Love hath been,
Shirîn, shirîntar, and shirîntarîn!" [1]

"Oh, Rose and Nightingale!" the Sultan said
"There shall be raised a white shrine to the Dead;
Where Love shall have — in garden fair and green. —
His endless song *Shirîn, shirîntarîn!*"

Shabash! we cried. By this the Mirza's nose
Bestrid with glasses, hung above the script:
His finger with the Meccan turquoise-ring
Guiding those mild worn eyes along the page.
Staid he commenced:

MIRZA. This volume of our Lord,
The Shaikh Muslihu-d-din Shirâzi, named
Sa'di, (may rain of Allah's mercy fall

[1] Persian for "Sweet, sweeter, sweetest."

Ever upon his grave!) the great Bostân,
Openeth full nobly, having entrance-porch
Like to yon stately doorway of the Taj,
Reared of fair stones, and rich with pious verse —
Wherein he telleth us of heavenly things,
And ways of Allah (be His rule extolled!)
This will I read, and, afterwards the Ishk:
Bi nama e Khudâ, so it preludeth,
The Gateway of the Garden of our Lord.

[*The* MIRZA *reads.*]

IN NAME OF GOD! Who maketh life to live;
Of God All-wise, Who speech to tongue did give;
Of God most Bountiful, Whose hand upholdeth,
Whose mercy doth th' offender's plea receive;

KING OF ALL KINGS, at Whose wide Palace-door
Who enters not finds majesty no more;

For, in that Court, the stiff-necked Lords of realms
Lie low and crownless on His praying-floor!

He doth not all at once the sinful slay,
Nor drive repentant runagates away:
Albeit an-angered at thy evil doings
When thou didst turn He did thy doom unsay.

Yet, in the ocean of His knowing, we
And all the worlds are bubbles of a sea;
He spies a fault, and spares it. If a son
Should vex his sire, hard would forgiving be!

And if a kinsman with his kin contends,
He spurns them, calling them no longer friends:
Nay, and thy slave — grown old and out of use —
The past good service no more recommends:

When those that had thy heart seem no more dear
Better a league away, than living near!
And if a soldier break his banner-oath
The Sultan from the roll his name will tear.

But He, the Equal Lord of low and high,
Doth to no sinful one His grace deny:
Ever He spreads His Adeem[1] *o'er the Earth,*
His Tray is full for friend and enemy.

Yet, had He willed, in way of might, to slay
Where liveth foe would be alive this day?
Above our hatreds, and unlike our loves
He ruleth! Jinns and men touch not His sway!

His Angels order Man and Bird and Beast,
The Fish, the Flies, the largest and the least;

[1] A tablecloth of painted leather used by grandees.

So plenteous is His bounty that the Ant
Finds meat, the vast Simurgh[1] *of Kâf can feast!*

Goodness and gifts diffusing, feeding these,
Because He is creation's Lord, and sees
All living things; and Solitude and State
Are His; and His Kingships and Dignities!

He sets on this man's head a golden crown,
And drags to dust from Empire that one down;
On this man's brow He binds good fortune's turban,
And round the other wraps misfortune's gown.

He makes the flames a Bower of Gulistan
For Ibraheem,[2] *but Farûn and his clan*
Hurls down to Hell by water; and both deeds
Are good, being the word of His Firmân.

[1] A fabulous bird which consumes forty bullocks at a meal.

[2] Alluding to the legend that when Abraham was cast into a furnace by King Nimrûd, Allah changed the fire to a garden of red roses.

What's covered He discerns, and what He will
He Himself covers of the acts done ill;
But, when, incensed, He bares the Blade of Judgment,
The Angels veil their ears with wings, and thrill.

Yet, when from off that Table of His grace
He gives what each may carry to their place
Azâzîl's[1] *self draws nigh: "Even for me*
A portion will be portioned!" Shaitan says.

Pitying sad hearts as Maker, Friend, and Guide;
Hearing all prayers which rise on every side;
With searching vision seeing times to be,
Acquainted with the shameful things we hide:

Lord of the Heavens above, and Earth below,
Lord of the Last Account! Each neck must bow

[1] The devil.

In deep submission to Him: hold not up
Finger of blame at His decreeing — thou!

All-good, All-True, His Reed of Destiny
Drew in the womb the earliest lines of thee;
He set the Sun and Moon from East to West
Speeding; and bent the blue arch o'er the Sea.

When Earth, bewildered, shook in earthquake-throes,
With mountain-roots He bound her borders close;
Turkis and ruby in her rocks he stored,
And on her green branch hung His crimson rose.

He shapes dull seed to fair imaginings;
Who paints with moisture as He painteth things?
Look! from the cloud He sheds one drop on ocean,
And from the Father's loins one drop He brings; —

And, out of that, He forms a peerless pearl,[1]
And, out of this, a cypress boy or girl;
Utterly wotting all their innermosts,
For all to Him is visible! Uncurl

Your cold coils, Snakes! Creep forth, ye thrifty Ants!
Handless and strengthless He provides your wants
Who from the "Is not" planned the "Is to be,"
And Life in non-existent void implants.

Again, He bids the embodied disappear,
And — shrouding it — to the Assembly-place doth bear
The Maidan of His judgment. Ah, we know
His Majesty and Might, but win not near

The secret of His mandates! nowise reach
What lies beyond all wit and sight and speech!

[1] It was a Persian belief that pearls were generated from rain-drops enclosed in sea-shells.

On that lone Peak perches no bird of Fancy,
No hand to touch the coasts of Him can reach!

A thousand ships have foundered here before,
So lost, no chip of them came back to shore :
I, too, on those waves wandered—many a night!
Till Terror plucked my sleeve, crying : "No more!

"To land!-th' horizon of God's knowledge rings
Thee and the worlds! think'st thou that King of Kings
To compass by conjecture? thou, a point!
When Wisdom's self wists not His hidden things?"

Hadst thou a tongue of wonder like Subhân[1]
It could not tell one Alif of the plan :
Rash horsemen on this road have spurred their coursers,
At La ahsâ[2] *they stopped, and sought the Khân!*[3]

[1] A very famous Arab poet and rhetorician.

[2] Meaning "I have not (adequately) praised Thee;" a verse of the Koran.

[3] The inn.

Since ways there be which not the stoutest ride:
Dark defiles where men fling their shields aside:
The Angels shut the gateway of returning
On whomso such far journey doth betide!

Who sits at banquet of such mystery
Must quaff a cup of senselessness. Oh, Sea
Of Fear never yet rounded! Landless ocean!
Wise pilots will not venture upon thee!

The long-winged hawk shall find his eyelids sewn!
The eagle, who with open orbs had flown,
His proud plumes singed. To treasures of Karûn
There was a path of going — not return!

Yet, in God's wilderness if thou wilt be
A traveller, untie thy camel's knee!
Dream not of home and friends! Thyself and Thou,
Mirror and face — that 's all the company!

Haply the fragrance of Heaven's hidden Rose
Hath maddened thee with love; thou art of those
Who tread the pathway of the Compact[1] *— searchers*
Waiting to hear the Voice. Truth will disclose

The Light — will rend the Veil of Flesh aside;
Except His glory nothing else shall hide!
Nothing! but wonderment must seize thy bridle,
Crying to Reason's horseman "No more ride!"

SAHEB. Noble! Janâb-i-Mirza! Yet, methinks,
There follow two more couplets — which begin
Dar in bahr, honoring your Prophet?

MIRZA. Yes!
I did not wish you should hold Sa'di stern
To "people of the book" other than ours;
Yet, of a truth, he ends the "Gateway" thus —

[1] Alluding to the story that, at the creation of living things, Allah asked them aloud: "Am I not your God?" to which all the elect replied: "Yea, Lord," thereby binding themselves forever to Him.

[*The* MIRZA *reads.*]

Over this Deep of God only one came,
Muhammad! If men follow not the same
Lost are they! Those that turn from following
Wander full far, and win distress and shame.

If, choosing other ways, Man thinks to gain,
He shall not to his journey's end attain.
Sa'di, speak truth! the Path of Purity
Only behind God's Chosen opens plain!

SAHEB. Be sorry for us, Gulbadan! and you,
Light-hearted Dilazâr! We shall not climb —
If this be sooth — into sweet Paradise,
Nor pluck the Tooba-tree, whose fair fruit bends
Glad to the hand; nor taste celestial wine
Sealed with the musk; nor ever see you wave
Green 'kerchiefs to us, 'midst those Heavenly ones —

Since Hûris you will be, with black-pearl eyes,
Lulu-l-maknûn! —

DILAZÂR. Did not the Mirza read
Azâzil's self comes to the Tray of God
And finds a portion?

GULBADAN. Oh, no need to leave
Our Saheb to Shaitan for his company!
There will be kind souls in Jehannum, Dear!
When I tied on the bells a Mollah said
There was no paradise for dancing-girls;
But one, well learnèd too, laid gentle hand
Upon his skirt, and answered: "Knowest thou this?
Hast thou, my Brother! keys of Heaven and Hell,
When the great Book saith (*Sura* Fourth it was!):
'Allah doth justify whomso He will;
None shall be wronged one date-stone'?" Who can tell?
We know not!

DILAZÂR. True, we know not! yet 't is sad

The Saheb should live a Kafir, loving so
Us and our people.

GULBADAN. Well! last year, in the Rains,
Our taïfah to Calcutta went, and I
Fell sick of country fever. — Dilazâr!
You cannot think how the blood runs all flame,
How bad the beating at the temples is,
And what fierce thirst! But, when I lay at worst,
There came an English Hâkimi to me —
A woman — wise, oh, as no Mollah is,
With pale face like the Saheb's, and eyes more blue
Than Mirza Hussein's ring-stone. Never a word
Questioned she of my faith, nor of my trade,
But — as we had been sisters of one womb,
Not fearing my wild speech, not hating me,
Foul, miserable, ill-ordered — bathed my brow
With sweet refreshing waters; cooled my mouth
With sherbets delicately mixed; combed smooth
My tangled hair, and sponged my burning skin

With touch more soft than ever lover had;
Then changed my cloth, and drew the chuddar straight,
Gave me some sovereign drug, and kissing me,
Said, "You will sleep, and will be well again
In time to dance, my Sister!" And I slept,
Dreaming so placidly of winds that blew
Wave-cold over the sea, fanning my face;
Of streams that ran snow-chill over my feet,
Calming my blood; — but, when I woke, and laughed
For comfort of glad life made new again,
There were my Hâkimi's kind eyes once more
Beaming, while 't was her white hands washed my feet,
And sprinkled fragrant essence on my brow
Rose-breathed! and, will you think I tell you truth,
Oh, Dilazâr! oh, Mirza? at her side, —
Come there to see us in the Hospital —
The high Lord Viceroy's wife, with gentle looks
And quiet voice, commanding all around;
Such a great "Mem-Saheb" that I drew my sheet

Lest she should see me and think scorn of me—
Lady Duffreen, the mighty Queen's Vice-queen!
Think, Dilazâr! and I a singing-girl!—
But, when I heard her speak soft Urdu words,
Like a white angel in her pity of us,
No whit afraid of *sitla*, or of *tap*
Fever or pest! there, for the love of us,
Pacing among the charpoys of the ward,
Followed by all the eyes with praise and thanks,
I turned my chuddar back to gaze and gaze:
And then I said—I think she heard me say,
My Hâkimi—"Ah, Mollah! if there be
No place in Paradise for Nautchenees,
We shall meet these, and that will not be Hell!"

DILAZÂR. Dear Gulbadan! how sinful, if they knew!
You should have whispered it, lest Kafirs heard
A Mussulmâni say so!

SAHEB. I rejoice
You saw our good and dear Vice-queen, who loves

Her Indian sisters, and makes help for them.
But this is not that Sa'di we should read.

MIRZA. I deem not so! Lord Sa'di speaks of Faith
At outsetting, since *Shariyat* comes first
In Sûfic lore, where forms and creeds are all;
Tarîkat next, when forms and creeds recede,
And "the Path" mounteth to *Hakîkat* free,
The Stage of Truth, past doctrines and past names,
And thence to *Ma'arifat*, the Stage Divine
Where the Soul dwells in light unspeakable;
Nor sees alone *Jalâl*, the Glory of God,
But *Jamâl* — Beauty, Grace, and Joy of God,
For which dear splendors we desire Him most,
Not for His Terrors, nor His Majesties!
And this dóth Sa'di inculcate in verse.
Nay, ye began him better than ye knew,
Speaking large charities, and hopes for all:
Since — writes he not? — Allah hath made us all
Angels, and Men, and Jinns; Birds, Beasts, and Fish;

And all are pictures from His hand; are cups
Filled with His wine; are steps to bring to Him;
Are whispers of the wonders of His Love!
Hear now *Khush-wakt*—how God's true lovers live:

[*The* MIRZA *begins the* ISHK.]

FAIR GO THE DAYS of them that drink Love's wine
Mighty and maddening! 'Tis a bliss divine;
Whether they suffer Separation's anguish
Or taste Propinquity's sweet medicine!

Earth's kingdoms shunning, these true Sultans be!
Rags of the Prison wearing these pass free
In changeless royal robes invisible,
For union's sake enduring poverty.

Time after time is shed into their cup
The bitter juice of pain—they drink it up,

And — if they find it sharp — 't is but to draw
Hard breath and wait, till better comes to sup.

Hides not the purple pleasure of the grape
Head-sickness underneath it? Can one 'scape
Wounds in the green Rose-garden, when no Rose
But arms with thorns her beauty? So, they drape

Their souls in dress of Patience! Patiently
Waiting for Love is well-at-ease to be!
Tani az dast-i-dost, — *oh, bitterness*
Comes sugared, when a dear hand gives it thee!

They see not — seek not — any drawing back;
Caught in this snare no captive asks to slack
His welcome chains! Rich mendicants, veiled monarchs
They know Heaven's Road, though ye note not their track!

Intoxicate with draughts of Heavenly love
They drink it deeper, while their smiles reprove
Our sober blame. Ah, have ye marked how lightly,
Drunken with desert-flowers, the camels move?

How shall men follow in the path they tread?
It runs in darkness like the crystal shed
By Life's hid River: like the Holy Houses
Outside all's blank, within is goodlihead!

Moth-like they flutter back into the ray
Which scorched them; silk-worm-like they spin away
This World's thread for the next World. Naught so fair
As to seem fair enough! If one should say,

Clasping his Heart's Delight, "Now, where is she?"
So are these always seeking! On the sea
They search for boundlessness; drinking Nile River
They ask, with parched lips, "When will water be?"

Sûfis! Heaven's chosen these! Oh, Adam's Son!
That lov'st another like thine own self—one
Built of the water and the clay—she also
Ravishes comfort from thee; all undone

Thou liest awake, for sake of mole on cheek,
Brain-sick, enamoured! And when eyelids seek
To drop sleep's curtain, all thy dreams are bound
In thought of her; of her thy lips still speak!

Beneath her feet, fond Votary! thou dost lay
Thy head submissive, in such lowly way
As if this Earth with all it holds were nothing,
And Joy bloomed only by her kindling ray.

Thy gold shows dim except she sees it gleam,
Otherwise gold and dust the same things seem:
Save for her kiss, thou sayst, how feel desire?
That such another breathes thou wilt not deem.

By day 't is "Apple of my eye!" by night —
When eyes are closed —'t is "Rest, thou dear Delight!
Sole in this heart!" No wandering wish, for shame!
No power, no will to win one hour's respite!

If she should crave thy life, to take away,
Thy life upon her hand thou 'lt haste to lay!
If she should bare a sharp blade for thy neck,
Joyously wouldst thou kneel that she might slay.

Lovers! whose love is fed on eyes' desire,
If this can so content, control, inspire,
Marvel ye that the wayfarers towards God
Plunge in Truth's ocean, burn with Frenzy's fire?

Passionate for the Unseen, as never none
Passioned for Seen; remembering — every one —
Day-tide and night-tide, only Him, as never
Lover remembered mistress under Sun!

For glee of God knowing no want or will;
World-heedless; seeing—whatever vintage fill
Earth's jewelled Cup—the Cup-bearer so splendid
That, all for ecstasy, His wine they spill!

Nor shall ye ever make them whole again;
Nor help with simples, knowing not their pain:
They hear you not; they only hear their Maker
Say, "Am I not your God?" piercing and plain,

For ever and for ever—as at first;
And clamorous answers from their being burst
"Yea, Lord! yea, blessèd Lord!" a crowd of Lovers
Outwardly humble, of the proud accurst,

But noble inwardly! Feet deep in mire,
But faces bright, eyes lit with astral fire:
Plucking the mountains from their roots with praying,
Piling great cities high with strong desire!

Wind-like they move at speed invisible;
Stone-like they testify, yet nothing tell;
Weeping by daylight, so that wild tears wash
Sleep's soorma from their lids! And night knows well

How these have urged the foundered Steed of Flesh
From watch to watch with meditations. Fresh
Breaks the gold-dappled Dawn to find them sighing
"No rest to us!"—for borne along in mesh

Of fiery phantasy they take no heed
If day or night be; notice not, indeed,
Whether sun shines, or stars or planets glitter:
So lost in Life they have forgot life's need;

So deep enamoured of the Picture-Maker
Who paints the face of Nature, that they take her
As naught—despite her gladness, wealth, and beauty—
And for His perfect sake wholly forsake her.

Yea! for they will not give to Forms their mind;
And if a fool gives, he is rash and blind!
Who scorns this for the next world, that man tasteth
True wine of Oneness — he of human kind!

SAHEB. Ah! but how far we seem from earth herein!
Above your topmost notes, fair Gulbadan,
Even if you sang on terrace of the Taj;
Beyond Dilazâr's reach, though she should dance
A-tiptoe in her little tinselled shoes,
And hold tamboora up at fingers' ends!
Can men, indeed, live on such cloudy food?
Must we not love the form, the grace we see,
The wine poured forth, the picture painted us?
Bring Sa'di down, Mirza! to Arjamand,
And flesh, and blood, and earth, — if that may be!
MIRZA. Sir! when you came, a second time, to see
This Taj, you mounted on the outer gate
Writ with stern Scriptures: and from highest roof

Marked the full greatness of the Tomb, far-off,
How its pale dome hung beauteous in the sky,
And how its white feet in these flowers were set,
Linking the Heaven and Earth in harmonies.
So is it here! Sa'di shows love of Heaven
Linked with the Earthly love, fulfilling it:
And how that beauty is of God at last!
Oh, you of Dihli! 'mid your lightsome lays
Know you a graver string-verse, can you sing
Shukur-i-Dost — the "Praises of the Friend"?

GULBADAN. Say me the line, Sir! Ah, yes! *Dil-i-man!*

[*She sings to a solemn air,* DILAZÂR *striking only the brass wire.*]

My heart I cannot fitly raise;
I know no language for His praise!

He gave me every hair that grows;
How thank Him, then, for each of those?

How bless enough, when I must bless
The grace to bless such blessedness?

Was it thy dam, or was it He
Made the soft womb to shelter thee?

And when they cut the cord, prepared
Tender true arms to be thy guard?

Soft bosoms, milkful, to arise
Like fountains filled from Paradise?

The mother, like a tree, to stand
Fruit on the branch, babe in the hand?

Life-giving and life-cherishing,
Feeding thy flesh from Love's own spring?

From breasts and veins that richly ranged
With blood which Love to nectar changed.

Whose was that wisdom? whose that plan?
Whose that sweet stratagem? oh, Man!

And this new neck of Mistress dear,
Didst thou devise, or find it here?

Did she and thou invent those eyes
Shedding such lustre, that surprise

Of Love caught up thy soul again,
Re-mounting on thy heart to reign?

But, thinkest thou He hath not thrifts
Of giving better than these gifts?

Deem'st thou He is not more to love
Than loveliest things below, above?

No "He"! — no "She"! but Twain! but All!
The Best, Last, Most, which can befall.

Ah! if that Mother's lap was warm
Wilt thou not trust th' Eternal Arm?

Ah! if the lip beloved was bliss
Wilt thou not woo celestial kiss?

Man! if stars gleam upon thy clay,
Wilt thou not sleep and wait His day?

SAHEB. What! can you dance to *Lála rukshar*, girl!
Or *Shukar lab*, and make great eyes for gain,
Knowing such strains?

DILAZÂR. Huzoor! we only are
Little green parrots, taught to speak our best:
You pay us with some sugar-cane,—and go,
Forgetting if our necks were red or gold,
Or if we ever lived.

GULBADAN. And, Saheb! bethink!
There was a great Lord in a garden found
A broken vase which smelt of nard and musk
Full sweet—and, when he asked "*Bû chist?*"—
Art thou
She whom the bulbul lauds for odorousness?
The potsherd meekly spake: "Sir, no such thing!
No Rose am I, but with the Rose I dwelled!"
So is it with thy servants!

SAHEB. Sisters, nay!
For Sa'di sings ye too are dear to God:
But, Mirza! make us hear what Sa'di says:

MIRZA. Now will he tell how even Earthly Love
Hath its persistence; and the might of that
To shòw self naught, leading the Spirit on
That it may lose itself, and gain by loss:

[*The* MIRZA *reads.*]

Once on a time, I heard, a Beggar's son
Loved — heart and soul — a Palace-nurturèd one;
Nursed the vain passion, till his wistful fancy
Plunged its teeth daily to Desire's bone.

Rooted he stood, like milestone, on the plain
Where she should pass; and, when she came again,
The Fil's not closer to the ivory Asp[1]
On play-board, than to her that love-lorn swain!

For her his blood to his pale cheek went leaping;
Foot-fast in mire of grief, he tarried weeping:
The Sultan's guards, observing this behavior,
Gave warning: "Be not found in these parts, creeping!"

[1] The "elephant" and "horse," two pieces of the Persian chess-table.

Awhile he fled; then, memory of her face
Returned resistless! In the self-same place
Anew he camped, beside her high pavilion.
A palace servant brake his head: "Disgrace

Be on thee!" cried he, "Spake we not, no more
Trouble us here?" Yet, still, as theretofore,
Patience and Rest remained not; that fair visage
Kept Rest and Patience from his spirit's door.

As flies are brushed from sugar, so they drove
This Lover off; and, still at speed, for love,
As flies come back to sugar sate he steadfast,
Heeding no blows. Him roundly to reprove

"Ai Shûkh! Dewâni-rang!" *one spake in scorn,*
"*Insolent Madman! truly thou hast borne*
Too patiently plain speech of stones and staves!"
He said, "This maketh me no whit forlorn!

"This cometh from the tyranny of one
Whose will is sweet! With Lovers surely none
Shall dare complain of what Love's hand inflicteth;
I breathe true breath of friendliness — alone,

"If that must be! — but, whether holdeth she
This faithful heart her friend or enemy,
Comfort is nowhere else, far from her presence
Patience hath never possibility!

"Too full of love my soul is to find place
For fear or anger. Dwell I here in grace
Or fly with foot of shame, here must heart linger;
Say thou not therefore 'Turn aside thy face!'

"'Quit the King's door!' No! not if they surround
My neck with cords, as peg of tent is bound;
No! the burned moth is happier in the lantern
Than live, and in the dark!" — The attendant found

This answer: "What if they shall beat thee black?"
The Lover said: "Ball-like I will roll back
At her dear foot!" Quoth he "But if they slay thee
With sharp of sword?" The Lover said: "Good lack!

"Then will I die, not grudging! Unto me
If nigh my neck gold chain or steel axe be
Full little knowledge is! but this is certain,
Idle it were to chide my ecstasy:

"Love finds no measure! If mine eyes were grown
Clouded with tears of woe as Yakûb's own
Still would I trust for sight of Yusûf![1] Lovers
Must not for every little let make moan!"

DILAZÂR. I could not love so!

SAHEB. Not if you were loved?

[1] The legend is that the eyes of Jacob became blind with weeping for Joseph.

DILAZÂR. *Afrîn!*[1] I might feel pity then, perchance;
And more, if — humble to the dust for me —
He had been bolder with those Palace-guards,
Stabbed the King's Muhtasib, and then sunk dead —
Covered with loving wounds, like rose-buds blown —
Or near to die, at lattice of my stairs:
Truly, if he were young and fair, with this
I might have softened, stealing down unveiled,
And kissing him to health with honeyed verse.

SAHEB. Would verse do that?

DILAZÂR. Why! Mirza Hussein knows
How in Lord Sa'di's time one little verse
Restored a dying Lover. He was fall'n
In death-trance at the door-way of his Love,
A princess proud and fair; but, as he sank,
He spake to such as gathered, lending help,
Three verses and one word — and they were these:

[1] A Persian exclamation of pleasure or admiration, meaning "Create!" *i. e.*, "Oh, Allah, make more like it!"

"Bring my Life, my Mistress, here!
Let her see me on my bier!
If she deign my lips to kiss
I ——[1]

"I" — then he swooned and spake no further thing.
But Sa'di, passing, questioned of the youth
Who lay so pale and still: — and when they told
How at that fourth line Silence stopped his tongue,
And when they said his sad words o'er again,
Sa'di fulfilled them, adding to the "I" —
"Shall rise! have ye no fear!" and so they brought
That Lady, and recited what had been:
Whereat, with pearls of pity on the leaves
Of those red roses blushing in her cheek,
Full tenderly she stooped — shame quite ashamed —

[1] The Persian lines were —

Janan-i-man baman biyarid
In mudah tanam bâdo miyarid
Agar boosa zanad bar in labânam
Ta ——
(*Sa'di filled in:* zindah shavam! ajab madarid.)

And kissed his mouth; and then the dead man rose,
Won back to happy days by lips and verse:
Much virtue lives there in a kiss and verse!

MIRZA. Yes! it so happened, Dilazâr; but here
Our Lover who is shadow of the Soul,
Straining for Beauty out of sight and reach,
For Love by perils girt, Joy walled by griefs,
Cometh not nearer than words far away
And worship strong as death. Attend again!

[*The* MIRZA *reads.*]

It chanced one day he kissed her stirrup-string;
Incensed, she flung aside! He said this thing,
Low sighing: "Nay! but do not draw thy bridle
The Sultan's self scorns no man worshipping.

"I am not I! 'T is thou art I and thou!
My Being is thy Being! Seeing thee now

What I was I forgot! No more reproach me,
Blood of my veins, and eyebrows of my brow!

"I touched thy stirrup with that hardihood
Taking no count of self! 'T is understood,
Naming thy sweet name blots my sad name out!
What thou wouldst be and have, is what I would!

"If thou wilt slay, the anger of thine eye
Sends death enough! No need, if I must die,
To strike! Set fire unto this bending reed,
And pass! All will be ashes by and by!"

SAHEB. Whither would Sa'di lead us, singing this?

MIRZA. Sarkar! the Poet leads us — as I think —
To this chief wisdom: that Love is not Love
Except it tear forth Self-love from the breast,
And so absorb the Lover in that frame
Of imaged fairness, where he finds soul's lamp

So draw, and daze, and tangle him with beams
(Ever so darkly radiating from God),
Beams all for him — albeit dull and dim —
That he shall quite forget what else was dear,
Wealth, comfort, peace, pleasure — nay, life itself —
To live and die in light of those bright eyes,
In reach of those sole arms, in blissful range
Of music echoing from that one sweet mouth.

DILAZÂR. Oh, Mirza! may I be your sacrifice!
But in what market does one buy such love?

MIRZA. In all the markets, Daughter! where they sell
Black snow, cold fire, dry water, and such goods;
For this thing cometh not of golden gifts,
Nor marriage-brokers, nor with bartered hearts,
But is by Kismat and the grace of God,
And bringeth where He will.

SAHEB. And, if He will
That it bring far?

MIRZA. Then may the Lover learn

Infinite things beyond that thing he sought:
For Beauty is a perfectness of Allah,
Showing Himself; and the Soul — seeing this
By vision of the senses, so devised
That flesh must thrill, delighted blood must course,
Heart bound with worship, and glad eyes grow dim
Beholding Beauty — Soul, perceiving this,
Hath first the impulse to create in turn —
Whence human crave for household, wife, and child,
Whereby this earth is peopled — then, past that,
The passion to draw near Heaven's perfectness,
To lose the Self therein, to live for it,
To win to wonders of the Rose-garden,
To secrets of the songs of nightingales
(Hark! do we know how Heav'n hath taught them
that?);
To silver meanings of yon midnight moon,
To reasons why honey is sweet, and musk
Fragrant, and skies so blue, and singing dear;

To hidden mysteries of Allah's love.
For more than He is glorious He is dear,
More than almighty sweet and beautiful,
(*Astaghfiru 'llah!* may Hẹ pardon this!);
Led so by spell of Love — be it for high,
Be it for low, whether 't is Arjamand
Worthy to lay a king's head on her knees
And teach him tasks, or some black hamâl's wench
Whose shining shoulders strike the simple heart,
So led, the Lover hath his man's blood changed —
In base hearts little, in the gentle much —
To mildness as of maid, to peace, to grace,
To sacrifice, and amity, and thirst
For manful deeds, that each may show himself
Grand in the eyes divine of what he loves.
For souls spread forth their purples and their gold
Peacock-like, in the sight of what they woo,
And even the slave is lordly where he loves.
Thus haps it that the breasts of Beauty nurse

Spirits to second life as mother-breasts
Nourished the babe to growth of boy and man;
So falls it — Sa'di means — that, lost in love,
The heart's-foot walketh yet a rightful path,
And all is wasted well for sovereign Love!

DILAZÂR. Will men waste much for Love?

GULBADAN. Oh, Dilazâr!
Do we not know? If Hâtim Tai could give
His horse for honor, where 's the lover fond
We could not bring to prison-bread and chains?

SAHEB. What was it Hâtim did, my Rose-bodied?

GULBADAN. If I have leave, 'tis told of Hâtim, Lord!—
The Mirza knows — how once he owned a steed
Swift-flying as the driving cloud, night-black,
With neigh of thunder; scattering in his stride
The desert-stones, as that thou wouldst have asked
"Is this a hail-storm breaks?" So fleet a steed
Men said the wind lagged after him; the foam
Blown from his scarlet nostrils lacked full time

To fleck the dust ere those strong clattering hoofs
Passed forth from ear-shot. And the fame of this,
Of Hâtim and his stallion, came to Roum,
Into the Sultan's ear; for one had said,
"No man is like to him for open hand,
And nowhere such a horse to bear such man!"
Then to his Vazir spake the King of Roum:
"Claim without proof is shame! let people go
And ask that horse from Hâtim; if he gives,
On wish of friendly Liege, what best he hath,
Then shall men know that liberality
Rules perfect in his breast; but, if he grudge,
This talk o' the world is but a drum-skin beat."

So, to the tribe of Tai the envoy went
With ten to guard him; and at Hâtim's camp,
After long travel, and sore times of strait,
Late, on a night of evil weather, lighted,
As glad as who comes parched to Zinda's banks.

The Chief's green tents were pitched amidst the waste,
The herds were far, the grain sacks empty, guests
Nowise awaited. Not the less, with cheer
Goodly and free the stranger folk were fed;
Full trays were served under the sheltering cloth,
Roast meat and boiled meat, pillaw and kabâb:
Sweetmeats he tied them in their skirts, and gave
Cakes in their hands; and all night long they slept
Safe upon Hâtim's carpets. When 't was day
The Sultan's envoy spoke his Lord's desire,
Saying with honeyed phrase, as one afeared,
"Oh, Giver of the Age! whose fame flies wide
For lordliness of heart and open hand!
My master bids me ask thy steed from thee,
That wondrous horse, night-black, swifter than wind,
Which if thou givest, liberality
Rules perfect in thy heart, but if thou grudge,
He saith this talk o' the earth is drum-skin noise."

But while the Sultan's messenger said this,
With forehead on the tent floor, and fair words,
Hâtim sate mute, gnawing the hand of Thought
With teeth of Lamentation. Presently
Outbrake he: "Would to God, Friend of my Tribe!
Thy message had been uttered over-night!
The rain beat, and the torrents ran death-deep
Between my tents and where our pastures spread;
No ox, nor goat, nor camel was in camp;
What should I do? How could I, being I,
Suffer my guests to sleep all hunger-racked?
How could I, being I, whose name is known,
Spare what was dearest, honor being more?
Look you! that Horse — my Friend! my Joy! my
Wealth!
That Duldul, who could leave the hawk behind,
Between whose hoofs I slept as in safe tent,
Black as a starless night, with mouth of silk —
I killed him for your suppers, tell the King!"

But when the Sultan heard this thing, he cried:
"None is like Hâtim! I would pawn half Roum
To buy black Duldul's life for him again."

SAHEB. Thanks! Gulbadan! Will Dilazâr doubt yet
What men may do?

DILAZÂR. Oh, but for pride — yes! yes!
Or fame, or name, Asylum of the Time!
Only I wonder if we singing girls
Come nigh the grace of such grand giving-ways
Or live in reach of Sa'di's mysteries.

MIRZA. Well! hear how Sa'di still continueth,
For 't is a Dancer takes the parable:

[*The* MIRZA *reads.*]

I heard how, to the beat of some quick tune,
There rose and danced a Damsel like the moon,
Flower-mouthed and Pâri-faced; and all around her
Neck-stretching Lovers gathered close: but, soon

A flickering lamp-flame caught her skirt, and set
Fire to the flying gauze. Fear did beget
Trouble in that light heart! She cried amain.
Quoth one among her worshippers, "Why fret,

"Tulip of Love? Th' extinguished fire hath burned
Only one leaf of thee! but I am turned
To ashes — leaf and stalk, and flower and root —
By lamp-flash of thine eyes!" — "Ah, Soul concerned

"Solely with self!" — she answered, laughing low,
"If thou wert Lover thou hadst not said so.
Who speaks of the Belov'd's woe as not his
Speaks infidelity, true Lovers know!"

SAHEB. Now, Dilazâr! whilst the wise Hussein rests,
Dance us a dance like that moon-visaged one
To suit this night and make Self quite forgot,
And tread thy doubts, and mine, and all, to dust

With beat of feet as soft as Sa'di's verse
And measures of the Mogul time.

DILAZÂR. My Lord,
I fear the lamp!

SAHEB. See, we will set it back!
It shall not burn one leaf of our light flower.
Now make the pacing pea-hens envious!

DILAZÂR. If Gulbadan will sing!

GULBADAN. Would you have this?
A ghazal like the songs of Arjamand
When the green Garden had no milk-white Taj.
Maybe she ofttimes heard such even here,[1]

[1] THE IMPERIAL MUSICIANS. — "I cannot sufficiently describe the wonderful power of this talisman of knowledge (music). It sometimes causes the beautiful creatures of the harem of the heart to shine forth on the tongue, and sometimes appears in solemn strains by means of the hand and the chord. The melodies then enter through the window of the ear and return to their former seat, the heart, bringing with them thousands of presents. The hearers, according to their insight, are moved to sorrow or to joy. Music is thus of use to those who have renounced the world and to such as still cling to it."

"His Majesty pays much attention to music, and is the patron of all who practise this enchanting art. There are numerous musicians at Court, Hindus, Iranis, Turanis, Kashmiris, both men and women.

By moonlight, to the splashing of the jets,
And echo of the bulbuls clamoring.

MIRZA. Aye! and to cry of yonder little owl
Who, Mirza-like, mid all your heedless notes
Hoots "hoo-hoo-hoo!"[1] as who should say "He! He!
The Highest! only God is Beautiful!"

La haula wa la kuwatu — he sighed,
Illa bi 'llahi! "Only God is great!
No glory otherwhere!" Then, while he laid
The gôli on his pipe-bowl, and drew deep
The scented smoke bubbling through rose-water,
The Kashmir Damsel, smiling, loosed the shawl
Draped rich about her hips; set firm the flower
Ablaze in her black hair; salaamed, and swam
Into the Persian measure, waving hands,

The court musicians are arranged in seven divisions, one for each day in the week. When his Majesty gives the order, they let the wine of harmony flow, and thus increase intoxication in some, and sobriety in others." — *Ayn* 30 *of Akbar.*

[1] *Hú, i. e.,* "He," God.

And swaying lissome limbs, while Gulbadan
Sang to *Nishastah*, and the beat of feet:

[GULBADAN *sings while* DILAZÂR *dances.*]

All in a Garden fair I sate, and spied
The Tulips dancing, dancing side by side,
With scarlet turbans dressed;
All in a Garden green at night I heard
The gladsome voice of night's melodious Bird
Singing that "Love is Best!"

The shy white Jasmine drew aside her veil,
Breathing faint fragrance on the loitering gale,
And nodded, nodded "Yes!
"Sweetest of all sweet things is Love! and wise!
Dance, Tulip! Pipe, fond Bird, thy melodies!
Wake, Rose of Loveliness!"

"Yet," sighed the swaying Cypress, "who can tell
If Love be wise as sweet? if it be well
For Love to dance and sing?

I see — growing here always — year by year
The Bulbuls die, and on their grassy bier
Rose-petals scattering!"

All in that Garden green the Rose replied:
"Ah! Cypress, look! I put my leaves aside;
Mark what is 'mid this bush!
Three blue eggs in a closely-woven nest,
Sheltered, for music's sake, by branch and breast!
There will be Bulbuls! hush!"

All in that Garden green the Bulbul trilled
"Oh, foolish Cypress! thinking Love was killed
Because he seemed to cease!
My best Belov'd hath secrets at her heart,
Gold seeds of summer-time, new buds to start;
There will be Roses! peace!"

Then lightlier danced the Tulips than before
To waftings of the perfumed breeze, and more
Chanted the Nightingale:

The fire-flies in the palms fresh lanterns lit;
Her zone of grace the blushing Rose unknit,
And blossomed, pure and pale!

MIRZA. Listen! Once more the small gray owlet cries
"Hoo! hoo!" among the palm-tops, testifying;
And Sa'di winneth ye to larger Love:

[*The* MIRZA *reads.*]

It comes to me what a wise ancient told,
How one, with God's love drunk, went — lone and bold —
Into the waste, and, when his sire with anguish
Of separation — foodless, sleepless, old —

Reproached him, he replied: "From that dear day
When He who is the Friend to me did say,
'Mine own thou art!' by God! no earthly feeling
In this glad bosom found a place to stay:

"By God! since He His beauty hath made known,
All other grace is dream and shadow grown."
Nay! and he was not lost who left his people!
God found him; and he found his All, his Own!

Shunners of Earth there be beneath our sky,
Half angels, half wood-creatures, wild and shy;
Like those, they rest not from remembering Heaven,
Like these, by day and night from men they fly

Their spirits' function strong, their senses weak,
Foolish and wise by turn, maddened and meek;
Stitching sometimes a mosque-coat in the corner,
Burning sometimes their mosque-coats, if men speak;

For life no strife, for naught solicitude.
Their hearts a cavern where no steps intrude,
To Union consecrate; — and there they sit
Reason-reft, ear-stuffed unto whoso would

Bring counsel. Let them sit! No duck is drowned
In water! No Samundar[1] *yet was found*
Singed by a flame! Full-stomached, empty-handed,
Without a kafilah o'er the sands they're bound.

No expectation of the people's praise
Have these! Enough that God accepts their ways:
Enough He holds them dear, His Darweeshes,
Who without wool or waist-cord pass pure days.

Nay! and these saints are like good vines which spurt
Wine from blue grapes, with pleasant shadows girt;
Not like those others, dark with evil doings,
No blue about them save their Sûfi shirt!

Shut on themselves — oyster-like — low they lie;
Not foam-like, bubble-like, careering by
Upon the wave-top. Fear them, being wise!
Men-jinns they are, masked with humanity;

[1] The Salamander.

Not men of flesh and bone! In common mould
Strange spirits dwell! Before the mart's outsold
The Sultan buys what slaves he needs: the tailors
Stitch clothes, but not the Sûfis whom they fold.

If white pearls grew from all the hail that fell,
Bazaars as cheap as cowries might them sell:
Oh! you shall seldom see those friends of God;
For over-gadding they are not shod well!

Companions of retirement, they hear
From Allah's lips the challenge high and clear,
"Ye! am I not your Lord?" One breath of that,
One draught from Heav'n's hid Love-cup, rich and dear,

Hath left them drunken, till, on Judgment-day,
Serâfil blows the trumpet. Threat ye may,
But edge of sword hearts' hold shall never loosen;
For, loosed—the glass would crack, faith fly away.

DILAZÂR. Your Sûfis sadden me! not flesh and blood;
Shy, desert-dwelling! I and Gulbadan
Could win from such no lovely gilded shawls,
No gulnàr-wreaths for neck and arms, no gems,
No clusters like to these — (Mirza Saheb, taste!)
Which hold the sunshine in their purple skins
And make wine lawful.

SAHEB. Shall they fetch you wine?

DILAZÂR. No! No! except Allah's wild wine of the grape!
We are good Muslim girls; we do not pour
Fierce liquors in our veins as I have heard
Feringhi ladies use, to graft, may be,
Red roses on the white silk of their cheeks.

SAHEB. Your ladies of great Akbar's court, 't is said,
And Shah Jahan's, sipped the forbidden juice;
And Hafiz' Tomb — think, Dilazâr, of that!
They show us at Shirâz the marble slab
Set fair over that dulcet Singer, laid

In alabaster 'mid his cypresses,
All writ with "perfumes and the wine-cup"—prayers
For "Minstrels" and the "Daughters of the Grape."

DILAZÂR. Oh, yes! we know; 't is *mazdah wasl*, Sir!
Reach me tamboora, Sister! it goes thus:

[*She sings the Tomb-song of* HAFIZ.]

"Comes then the message of Thy Love to me,
Bidding arise?
This bird, my Soul, yearns to be floating free
In Thy pure skies!

"Oh, call me but Thy servant, I will go,
Glad to be dust;
Higher than all desire of things below
In Love and Trust!

"Pour down upon me from Thy pitying cloud
Of Mercy fair
Thy Rain, that I may blossom from my shroud
In Heaven's high air!

"And ye, who at my Tomb sit, make no moan;
The wine-cups bring!
Bring flowers, and perfumes, and the lute's clear tone,
And those that sing!

"That my soul go a-tripping gay and fain;
Thou, Heart's Delight!
Though I be old, embrace me once again
For this last night!

"Kiss me a-dying! make me young once more!
Be thyself, Sweet!
That Hafiz, rising soul-reft from Earth's floor,
Go with glad feet.

MIRZA. Oh! *toba! toba!* that was Sûfic phrase
For wine of Love celestial, and far joys
Waiting the Faithful, if they hold true faith;
As he who wooed the maid of Samarkand
Whereof our Lord the Poet singeth next:

[*The* MIRZA *reads.*]

In Samarkand one loved a Mistress fair;
Not speech, but spoken honey thou wouldst swear
Flowed from her lips. Of beauty so transcendent
The Sun spent all his gold to gaze on her!

The corner-stones of continence were shook
Whithersoever her light glance did look;
Tâali Allah — *oh, by God the Glorious!*
Her face for Heaven's sweet mercy wise men took.

When she would walk abroad the eyes of all
Drew after her ensorcelled! Hearts did fall
Into her steps and follow! Lovers longed
To buy it with their blood, one hour to call

The Lady theirs: but this poor Lover worst
Burned for her; sent his sad eyes last and first
After her passing feet, silently glancing;
And so it chanced that, one day, she outburst:

"Ai Khîra-sar! *Perverse! Dost cast on-me*
Eyes of a hunter? I am not for thee!
No bird thy net can snare! Vex me no farther,
Or thou shalt taste knife-kiss of enmity."

Then some one spake: "Thou hearest? let her go!
Choose kinder fair! I think thou wilt not so
Assuage thy thirst of heart; and God forbid
Thou shouldst thy life stake on a quest of woe!"

But he — love-maddened, liver-saddened — heard;
Then from his soul's depths drew this patient word,
Saying, "Allow! with wound of sword or knife
She lay me corpse, by blood and dust besmeared,

"Will they not say — midst enemies and friends —
'Here's he that by her hand and dagger ends'?
How to desist I not one whit discern;
Urge not mere living makes Love's death amends!

"*Chidest thou me? repentance dost thou teach?*
Repent thyself! 't were better than such speech,
Self-seeker! Nay, but pardon! all she doeth
Excellent well is done, even if it reach

"*Unto my doom. Oh, I burn every night,*
Slain, moth-like, by her eyes; yet morning light
Makes me alive with lovely memory
Of musk and spice wherewith her hair is plight!

"*If then, to-day — or any day — I die*
In my Beloved's street, when times roll by
And Resurrection-dawn is come, consider
My tent to my Beloved's must be nigh!" —

Oh, Lover of the girl of Samarkand,
Shābash! *in strife of heart droop not the hand!*
Yield naught! at latest anguish Love attaineth.
Sa'di — whom Love slew — here alive doth stand!

SAHEB. Well! *Shabash!*—but, I wonder, did it please
That self-willed dame of Samarkand to know
He would be waiting for her, tent all pegged,
When great Serâfil sets the trump to mouth,
And graves are opened? Must a man in love
Never take answer when the answer 's "No"?

MIRZA. Not if he love as Sa'di meaneth love;
For underneath the scripture this intends
A soul set resolute to gain to God.

SAHEB. What say you — being woman — Gulbadan ?

GULBADAN. *Bi-Khuda*, Saheb! I say we are ill-pleased
When "No" can kill the seed of Love in men;
For "No" is oft-times woman's touchstone; "No"
Tries the false Love, but turns with true to "Yes."

DILAZÂR. There is that story of the maid of Marv
Whom one did follow, uttering earnest vows;
"Follow me not!" quoth she, "there comes behind
A woman beautiful as moon of spring,
I am but shadow of her face and grace!"

Whereat he turned, and did encounter so
A hag of ugliness, *zan-i-shaitan.*
Furious he comes again: "Why didst thou lie,
Crook'd Cypress of the grove?" he cries: but she
Laughed, and said lightly, "Lie doth warrant lie!
How couldst thou love me, when upon a "No,"
And promise of some fairer one, thy feet
Left following?"

MIRZA. There she answered well, methinks,
For even to fail of love is dear in Love,
Which Sa'di telleth us by what haps next.

[*The* MIRZA *reads.*]

One, perishing of drouth, even while he died,
"*Ah! to be drowned! — how good!*" *with parched lips sighed.*
"Ajab!" *a foolish friend returned —* "*I wonder,*
Being dead, what matters mouth moisted or dried?"

The sick man said: "It matters that at brink
Of Death I quaff and quaff, till Life's chin sink!" —
Yea, Brother! and, for this all thirsty Lovers
Plunge to Love's depths; they know that drowned men drink.

If thou be lover, grasp her skirt! loose not!
If she say "Die!" lay life down on the spot!
When thy feet pass o'er Hill of Non-existence,
Lovely surprises may become thy lot.

At seed-sowing the sowers' hearts are fain:
But when sheaves ripen they rest well again!
In Heaven's high banquet if Cup come to mouth
Only at last round, that's the last of pain.

SAHEB. Lofty the teaching is, and fair the verse,
Yet, in what world did learnèd Sa'di live?
Were all his ladies cold and lovers meek
As those of Samarkand? You, Rose-bodied!

Who have the voice — you, dark-browed Dilazâr!
Would hardly ask a man to die for you,
That somewhere, on the Hill of Nothingness,
"Lovely surprises might become his lot."

GULBADAN. *Ay-wai!* if we did ask, who would consent
To wait for us on that chill Ridge of Death
Where no hands clasp, and no lips are to kiss?

DILAZÂR. Were I a man, and loved so, I'd not die
Till he was dead who kept her heart from me
Or she that so denied it!

SAHEB. Why, see there!
Your black eyes flash with knife-blades! That's i' the blood,
To have the form we prize, and burn and rage
With jealousy to lose it, or to share.
Ask Mirza Hussein how he makes this good?

GULBADAN. Ask for us, Sahibâ! Feringhees know
So many books, Aflatûn, Aristû,
The windings of the ways of these dim things;

We are the fluttering birds who come to peck —
At evening, when the noisy world is still —
Crumbs of dropped wisdom.

SAHEB. Now the Mirza smiles!
Yet you, oh, Heart-destroyer! Dilazâr!
You must have heard and seen what Love I mean
Imperative, unswerving, desperate,
Not heedful of sweet Heaven which made things fair,
Not set to gentle notes of nightingales,
Not lapped in ruffled rose-leaves; but still "Love"
As the world names it, and some women deem.

DILAZÂR. I could recall a thing, if my Lords would,
Such as you say.

MIRZA. Yes! tell it, Dilazâr!
Sa'di will answer.

DILAZÂR. Presences! we camped
At Delhi, by the Kashmîr gate, for gain
And marriage-feasts, and doings of the Eed;
A Taïfah of eleven, with four who played

Sitar and drum; and one was Lakshmî named,
A brown Mahratta girl of high-caste blood
(I know not how she came to wear the bells)
Beautiful — Sirs! — like yon moon overhead,
And young, and yet unyielded — by some vow —
Dûr-i-na sufta, an unthreaded pearl!
We were commanded to a Palace-feast
Where round a gay ring sate the powerful ones,
Rajahs and Sirdars, in a cloistered court
Shining with lamps and fountains, and white gleam
Of marbles glistering; and your Sahebs were there,
Proud English officers, with cold blue eyes
Which look you through and through, and could look
down
The green balls of a panther in his spring —
One of them, proudest, handsomest; they said
He had slain nine in fight, and never yet
Bent knee to woman! Lakshmî went with us,
For, girl albeit, she danced as no one else
That Ras the Deccan favors, with high song

Where Krishna is the cowherd, and pipes sweet,
And one by one the timid milkmaids trip
To list, as in Brindâban once they did;
The snake-skin marking every subtle step.
Our best had played, but no man heeded them,
Rajah or Sirdar, least of all that Saheb
For one glance of whose lordliness we strove,
When Gunesh thumbed the bass Mahratta drum,
And Lakshmî let her chuddur fall, and stepped
Into the lamp-light, to the dancing-place.
You would not wonder, Huzoor! had you seen —
All started, but the English Captain most.
He gazed; played with his sabre-strap; and gazed;
And drew this way and that his golden beard;
And clasped his palms, as 't were some heavenly dream
So like a desert-deer she glided near,
So leaf-soft on the carpets fell her feet,
So perfect to the music moved her limbs,
So fair she was and winning, with no gems

Bound on her neck, no rings, no belt of gold,
Only her yellow choli and gauze skirt
And one red lotus in her glossy hair!

SAHEB. But, Dilazâr! you paint her with Love's brush!

DILAZÂR. I have no need! She was not good to me,
Wilful and wayward, with the Deccan blood
Which takes and gives not; yet bewitching, too,
A Neem-tree of the trees, a Palm for grace!
Dilburda — ah! a girl to steal the heart!
The rest you judge. She set his blood aflame
Before the second measure of the Song,
With what the Saheb speaks of, lightning-love;
And Lakshmî, like all women, saw and knew
As soon as he. So, when she danced his way
And finished at his side — with bended head
And little rose-dyed hands crossed on her breast —
All proud and cold and lordly as he was
We saw him loose the golden chain he wore
And knit it round her throat, whispering quick praise;

While Lakshmî kissed his hands, and from her hair
Plucking the lotus laid it at his feet.

GULBADAN. Naught hindered, then, that she should give him more!

DILAZÂR. Much hindered! for she hated—(pardon this,
My Lord!)—your Saheb Lók! One of her house
Perished in days of the great Mutiny,
Blown from the cannon's mouth: Lakshmî had heard
How bold he stood at those black lips of death,
And how the red flash leaped, the white smoke swept,
And what was living fearless Man became
A rolling turban, and torn twisting shreds,
Whirled in the bloody dust. Another thing!
Gunesh, who made the music, had her heart,
If there beat any heart in that cold breast.
Together in one village they had dwelled,
Playmates from birth, and promised each to each.
Therefore in vain the English Captain prayed,
In vain his strong neck bent at Lakshmî's feet!

Naught won he with that brown Mahratta maid
By gifts, or words, or honeyed messages,
Save "Never! never!" from sweet lips set close,
And looks from Gunesh fierce enough to kill.

SAHEB. I am ashamed my countryman so stooped!

DILAZÂR. Ah, *Gharib Purwar!* you have said; 't was Fate!
'T was that wild force which will not let us be!
Your countryman was high and dutiful
Till *Nuseeb* smote him with the dark girl's glance,
Then all was naught save Lakshmî. 'T is our way,
Nay! 't is our sin, which shall have punishment,
To know that this may be, and make it be.

SAHEB. I deem not love so blind, manhood so weak!

DILAZÂR. *Afsos!* it happens! He would ride, of nights,
Twenty-five koss to see her dance; would quit
His friends, his tasks, the race, the tiger-hunt,
If he might snatch one hour at dusk to plead
With Lakshmî for her love—yet all in vain,
Because of Gunesh, and her vow, and grudge

Stored in her veins against the Gora-Lók.
But one day came a Sonar, selling stones,
Nose-gems and ear-gems, *chatkis* for the toes,
Jasams for elbow-bands, and *gote* and *har*,
Bala and *mala;* and, when all were shown,
A string of great picked pearls, and two pearl-moons
Wrapped in a cloth. "See! I unroll you these
That you may dream you wear them!" mockingly
He said, and laid the milky luxuries
On Lakshmî's knee — "I have a prince will give
Rupees six thousand for that beauteous row:
Who wears it wears a *jaghîr* round her neck!"
Then Lakshmî's eyes lighted with leopard's gleam,
Her small brown eager hands fondled the pearls,
Twice round her throat she clasped the string and
sighed:
"Shiva! how beautiful: would 't were my Prince!"
And he was by, watching her ache for it.

GULBADAN. I guess your story now!

DILAZÂR. No! not its worst!

We were to journey next day northwards — far —
But that night, through the lattice of our hut
I saw his gold lace glitter, where she sate;
I heard his deep voice shake, while he said this:
"Lakshmí! without your love I shall not live:
Take from my soul the spell of those great eyes
Or heal their mischief with those flow'r-soft lips!"
But "*Denga nahin!*" she muttered, "Saheb, no!
My father's brother at the cannon's mouth
Had so much love as I will give to thee!"
And then he clinked his spurs, and whispered wild,
"Thou wilt not love me? black Mahratta witch!
Who hast the bosom of Heaven and heart of Hell,
Well! let me buy thee!" and therewith he flung
That milk-white lovely pearl-string in her lap,
Which coiled across the velvet skin like snake
White-bellied, shining, worming flickering road
Over dusk leaves, and like the subtle snake
Struck her, and stung that sullen soul with greed.

SAHEB. What! yielded she?

DILAZÂR. She had the Deccan itch,
That strain of Sivajî! I saw her play
Wistfully with the pearls; and then she plucked
Her temple-flower, the rose-red lotus-bud,
Forth from her hair, and flung it at his feet
With petulant quick cry, as once before;
And wound the white string back and forth in gleams
Amid her braids; and, letting loose the shawl
Tied round her waist, arose, made low salaam,
And beckoned him inside the purdah; still
Twisting those pearls tight in her untied hair.
I laughed and slept.

GULBADAN. Where, then, 's 'the worst' in this?

DILAZÂR. Herein! that Gunesh saw him come and go!
Next dawning, at what hour the 'Wolf's Tail' sweeps
The sky clear of late stars, in his own tent
That Saheb lay with proud heart still a-beat,
Musing on Lakshmî, and her dear-bought love.

'T was such a time as this — you feel how still!
Tethered close by the cattle shook their bells;
You heard them chew the fodder sleepily;
Far off the first crow cawed, winging for food;
The *Dam-i-subh*, soft Breath of Morning, shook
The flag at quarter-guard, and stirred the grass;
The tent-cloths flapped, the gray light crept and spread,
The jackals sniffed the coming day, and yelled:
A bugle of reveille blew! He rose
To cool his brow with kiss of morn: lo! there,
Face to face, at the entrance of his tent —
Set on a lance-staff planted in the sand —
Was Lakshmî's head! that rose-red temple-flower
Replaced amid her blood-stained braids, those pearls
Knotted upon her bleeding throat, the eyes —
Which were so lustrous — glazed and blank, the mouth
A-grin with Death's ill-laughter! Round the spear
Fluttered a paper written: "*Sahebji!*
You bought her false lips dear! have now, beside,

Head, neck, and all! with every hair a curse
On her, and you! — Gunesh, the Deccannee."

SAHEB. Aye, so! And what would Sa'di say of this?

MIRZA. Sa'di would say this was not Love at all,
But bitter Lust, which loves itself, and buys
Pleasure for self, at whoso's cost and pain.
The true Love riseth from dear Beauty seen —
By gentleness, submission, reverence —
To larger Beauty unbeheld; adores
The Painter in his picture; at cup's brim
Tastes wine, with heart fixed on the Cup-bearer,
Ever made kindly to the sweet thing loved.
The false love is, as these of Dilazâr,
Furious and pitiless in will to have,
Mean and unloving in the act to yield,
And savage in swift hate of what was prized;
The amouring of beasts that kiss with teeth!
Hear rather wise Lord Sa'di, in this verse
Which cometh from the honeyed *Gulistan:*

[*The* MIRZA *recites.*]

A Lover, with his loved One, sailed the sea,
Voyaging home in tender company:
There blew a wind of Death upon the waters;
There broke a billow of calamity!

It swept them from the deck to dreadful breast
Of the black ocean. To that pair distressed
The mariners flung forth a plank of rescue;
It reached them drowning on the tossing crest.

Too slender 't was to help — if both should hold;
They saw him round the plank her weak arms fold,
"Gîr! Dast-i-yar-i-man!" *he uttered softly;*
"*Clasp! hands! dearer than Life to me!*" *The cold*

Bitter salt swallowed him. But those who brought
His beauteous Maid, saved by that sweet deed wrought,

Spake, saying, "Never lived there truer Lover!
Majnûn by such a marvel had been taught!"

SAHEB. Your Shaikh Muslihu-d-din Shirâzi has
Fair meditations, Mirza! does it teach —
His "Garden" — why, in our mid hearts, we feel
'T was better for that faithful Lover dead
Than for Dilazâr's living?

MIRZA. Sir! it doth.
If we should measure bulk and wealth of bliss
As we mete grain or gold dust, he who sank
Tasted more perfect pleasure of the soul
In that one eager instant's sacrifice,
In that last worship of his Well-Beloved,
Choking with brine, buying her breath with death,
Than Lakshmî's Lover with his evil gift.
Oh! Sûfis know how dearer far than wine
The Tavern-Keeper is, how lovelier
Than any picture is the Painter's face!

And these two knew it, at whose graves we sit,
Arjamand, and the Emperor, who held
Love dearer than their greatness and their realms.
Can you sing *Mâlik budam*, Gulbadan!
If Dilazâr sings the Sultana's verse?

[GULBADAN *sings.*]

I was Sultan of Hind and the mountains;
Chenab and Ravee
Were mine, from their silver-white fountains
To the sands of the sea:
And Gunga and Jumna, with blisses
Of Lordship and Line;
Yet I counted them less than thy kisses,
My Lady divine!

[DILAZÂR *sings.*]

I had gold robes and greatness, and sweetness;
I was queen of the Land;
In my Palace shone pride of completeness;
On my lips sate command:

But the heart of my Lord was my glory,
Not the crown on my brows;
And my garden is green with Love's story,
And my Tomb is Love's House!

SAHEB. Thanks! Bulbuls of our Rose-grove! Now what next
Will the scroll say?

MIRZA. It turns to constant Faith:

[*The* MIRZA *reads.*]

I have a tale of them that go about
Treading God's road — rich beggars, kings i' the clout:
An old man 't was, wending at early morning,
Who spied a mosque porch, and he raised his shout.

Then, some one said: "Here 's not the People's Door,
Where they give anything; howl thou no more!"
The Ancient asked, "Whose is this Mansion, Friend,
Where they give nothing to Heaven's starving poor?"

He said : " Khamôshi ! *hush ! speak no rash word !*
The Master of this house is God the Lord."
The old man looked ; he saw Lamp and Mihrâb :
Forth from his liver this lament he poured :

" *Alack, alack ! I will stay here I trow,*
Alack ! if help befalleth me not so !
I came not forth from any street unpitied,
From God's door yellow-faced why should I go ?

" *Hand of entreaty will I stretch out here,*
That it come empty back I shall not fear."
Therewith he sate, sojourner, suppliant,
Lifting the palm of asking all one year.

At the year's end his foot of Life went low
Into Death's clay ; his heart beat fast and slow,
Drumming Departure's march. One held a lantern
At daybreak, scanning him. Faint as the glow

Of lamp-wick in the dawning, so his snuff
Of waning life still burned; from weasand rough
They heard him murmur: "Oh, at last it opens,
God's Gateway, if we beat it long enough!

"Sweet and submissive be His grace to win,
I never heard an Alchymist gave in;—
Look how he melts pure gold in th' alembic,
That one day, peradventure, brass begin

"To shine forth gold! And gold is good to spend
For fitting ends; and what were fitter end
To lavish gold and life and all for buying,
Than God the Lover's love, God's the great Friend?

"When by some ravisher of hearts thy heart
Is straitened, wise it were from such to part;
Another will console thee; unkind faces
Render days bitter! Cool the false fire's smart

"With dew of fresher lips! Lightly men quit
Love, when light need their spirits have of it;
But if She be beautiful past compare,
Then, for small griefs to go, that were unfit!"

SAHEB. I mark how steadfastly Sa'di will lift
Passion of Earth to Heavenly: we, too much,
Muse upon God as Glorious, Awful, Great
Majestic, Just, Holy, Inflexible,
Forgetting He is Beauty, Sweetness, Joy,
Desire, Delight, Fulfilment of all wish,
Is it not so?

MIRZA. Ay, Saheb! 't is so! *Jamâl*,
The grace of God — is greater than *Jelâl*,
Glory of God: but at the last these meet
In Love shown Power, and Power grown beautiful,
Pitiful, reconciling, ridding sins;
As shall be seen in this which followeth:

[*The* MIRZA *reads.*]

I heard that old One, all his night of woe,
Raised hand of need to Heaven devoutly so:
And some voice said again: "Profitless Fool!
Sar-i-Kwesh gîr! *Take thine affairs and go!*

"Thy prayer is unaccepted at this Door!
Depart rejected! trouble peace no more!
When thou hast seen Attention's Wicket fastened,
Prolong not uselessly a struggle sore!"

The tears which trickled down his aged cheek,
Had tinge of blood while his thin lips did speak:
"Ay, Gholam! hopeless had I turned away
And left this House some other house to seek:

"But if thy friend in wrath from thee doth snap
Bridle, wilt thou not seize his saddle-strap?
An asker, disappointed at one gateway,
Knowing another open hath good hap!

"Ye say my way is nowise in this street,
Yet nowhere else shines any chance so sweet;
Nowhere another Path, nowhere a Portal!"
With that his head upon the earth he beat.

And, suddenly, was whispered — as he died —
In his soul's ear, "Son, thou art justified!
Kabul ast! *'t is accepted! have thou comfort!*
Except in Us no comfort could betide!"

SAHEB. Yes! but how long he waited! this is hard!
Sometimes, perchance, we see and know how rich
That Unseen Beauty is; — but Heaven is far
And Earth is near! we beg in the next street,
We crave for passing hearts, not good to crave;
We knock at porches showing well outside,
Forgetting God's fair gate! Somebody gives!
We munch our crust of Love, and live! What good
To lie and die at door of Allah's house?

What strength, if there were good? since night must
come,
And cold and emptiness?

MIRZA. But after night
The happier day! Sing him the *yar-i-man*,
Those verses that the glad dead Minstrel writes
Of "Death and Darkness," Gulbadan! and then
I will read Sa'di.

[GULBADAN *sings.*]

Fear not the darkness, Friend and Lover!
The fount of Life ariseth there!
Rest comes when hope of Rest is over;
I suffered, but am happy here!

Consume thou not thy soul with scorning,
Because Desire found no allay:
Soon will there be bright birth of Morning
The Night is far gone with the Day!

MIRZA. True! had we never seen Day's miracle,
Who, looking eastward now of Mumtaz' Shrine,
Would dream glad Morning, 'neath yon silent stars,
Gathered her saffron sari to trip forth,
With sun for forehead-jewel? Man must wait,
And not "for every little let make moan!"
This will our Master's verses now impart:

[*The* MIRZA *reads.*]

A new-wed Bride, in tender discontent,
To One, gray-haired, made of her Lord lament,
Saying: "Thy son no praise from thee doth merit,
So cold he is, so ill my hours are spent.

"Those who with us in the same village dwell,
I never mark their looks of heart-ache tell;
Such close companions, man and woman, are they,
That thou mightst say, 'two almonds in one shell!'

"But I have never seen mine — all this while —
Gaze once upon my face with loving smile!"
The father, kindly-hearted, heard her speech;
The white-haired one her grief knew to beguile:

The answer which he gave was soft and sweet,
Saying, "He is so comely, it were meet
To love and wait, enduring till he love thee:
'Twere pity from such path to turn thy feet,

"Since nowhere in the world could any be
So dear, so near, so framed for unity." —
O Man! wilt thou be petulant with God,
Whose reed — if He were petulant with thee —

Blots out all writing of thy life? Obey!
Be still, and wait for word which He will say!
The Lord's time is the servants' time; and never
Another Lord like Him shall come thy way!

Once my heart burned in pity for a Slave,
Who at the selling-place this utterance gave:
"Ah, Master! Better bondsman thou mayst find,
But I no better Master e'er can have!"

SAHEB. Yet, none the less for that Slave's faithfulness,
His Master sold him!
MIRZA. Yea! and none the less
That Love which did forgive and cling to Love
Went with the Slave, and made him happier days,
Or stronger soul to bear the ill days. Sir!
It is not needful Love should win its wish
But only needful that it work its work.
Yon palms grew high striving towards the Sun,
They shall not reach him, but — uptending thus —
Leaves, flowers, and fruit have come! Past question, here
In this world, midway 'twixt the light and dark,
Much is to wish and wonder at: hearts play —

Like Akbar with his ladies — hoodman-blind
Among the courts and cloisters of our life:
They stumble, and they fumble, and go wrong;
Of this, moreover, doth the Master speak:

[*The* MIRZA *reads.*]

There dwelled in Marv a Hâkim, angel-faced;
His form, in Garden of the Heart, was graced
As is the cypress: yet he had not skill
To heal sick souls, nor know when passion's waste

Dimmed longing eyes. And some one — ill at heart,
Spake afterwards: "I had Love's bitter smart
For him! I wished not ever to be well,
Lest he should call me cured, and so depart." —

Much wisdom is there, hard to overthrow,
Which Love's strong sorcery can bring full low.
Hand of light Love, when it holds Wisdom's ear,
Makes Sense with muzzle in the dust to go!

DILAZÂR. If 't were a woman she had surely known!
Our sex owns one more sense than yours, my Lords!
'T is giv'n that we may read the hearts of men
Through thirty silences.

GULBADAN. But *did* he doubt?
There is a verse on that, in two soft parts,
When first the Lady, next the Lover speaks:
They sing it in the Afghan towns:

SAHEB. Sing now,
Nightingale of the Age!

GULBADAN. Hazrat! I shall,
If Dilazâr will tread the step, and say
The Lady's portion:

[*They sing, and* DILAZÂR *dances.*]

GULBADAN. I am sitting in sadness, deep-stricken
With a wound that is death,
If thou com'st not, Physician! to quicken
My soul with thy breath.

Have you seen, have you seen, oh my Brothers!
A Hawk flying south;
Blacker-plumed, brighter-eyed than all others,
With a heart in his mouth?

Ah! stay him! 't is mine, it is mine!
He has reft it amain!
I am red with Love's blood, with the wine
That is pressed from Love's vein.

DILAZÂR. My Belovèd hath breasts like pomegranates!
Her teeth are sea-pearls!
Her eyes shine with splendor of planets;
Like the tangled silk curls

The heart-net enwove by her tresses;
I fly with faint feet!
Oh, Allah! her clinging caresses!
Is Thy 'Garden' so sweet?

My Belovèd knows not how I love her,
That the sick one is I;
I escape, lest the patient recover,
And the Hâkim should die.

MIRZA. Vainly he strives to fly, if it be fate;
And fate comes, good or bad, by woman's hand
As judgment, too, must come by woman's mouth.

SAHEB. *Ajab!* how strange! a priest of Frangestan[1]
Wrote likewise in his glittering French, "That Day—
That Judgment-day — the sentences men hear
Will be the sentences pronounced on them
By women, countersigned of God the Lord."

DILAZÂR. Bi-Khûda! then how I will punish some!

GULBADAN. By great Jibrâil! how sweet to pardon, then!

MIRZA. Oh, but you also shall be then adjudged!
Our Lord the Prophet (peace be unto him!)
Recorded that of perfect womankind
Were never more than four — Asia the Queen
King Pharaoh's wife; Khadijah, Fâtima;

[1] "En somme, j'ai été aimé des femmes dont il m'importait le plus d'être aimé. . . . Ma part a été bonne et ne me sera pas enlevée; car je m'imagine souvent que les jugements qui seront portés sur chacun de nous dans la vallée de Josaphat ne seront autres que les jugements des femmes, contresigné par l'Éternel." — RENAN, "Souvenirs d'Enfance et de Jeunesse," p. 361.

And the Lord Isa's mother, Mariam.
But now will Sa'di warn ye in his verse
How hard to conquer is misguiding Love:

[*The* MIRZA *reads.*]

Was one that trained his sinews, day and night,
Meaning to grapple with a Lion's might;
He found his Lion — grappled — but he found
Scant strength, in such a deadly grip, to fight.

Quoth one who watched, "Dost sleep? art woman grown?
Strike him that blow of brass thou mad'st thine own!"
"Alas! it is not possible thereby
To conquer Lions!" — so they heard him moan.

With Wisdom — when False Love puts forth command,
'Tis as that Lion, and that hunter's hand!
No iron-grasp shall help thee, woman-weak;
Love's bat drives Reason's ball from stand to stand.

SAHEB. I see not Sa'di puts the case of him
Who loves aright, yet is not loved, and finds
No love elsewhere: for, surely, hard to tread
The heavenward way is, if no guide will lead.
Here in your East, you set the problem by
With marriage-brokers; or mate baby-hearts,
Which grow by stress of years and circumstance
To suit and fit like two nuts in one shell;
But in our West, where all are free to choose,
This pinches! One we honor for his songs —
Greater than Sa'di's self[1] — asks wistfully:
"*Of Love that never found his earthly end*
What sequel? streaming eyes and broken hearts?
And all the same as if it had not been?"

MIRZA. Naught is the same "as if Love had not been!"
Where it hath shone it is like sunlight poured
On seeds which slept, surprising naked soil
Into new verdure, and an unhoped Spring.

[1] Lord Tennyson.

Nor 'scape we, by our Eastern ways, those griefs
Springing from liberty. Yet reason tells
Who would be loved must needs show lovable,
Otherwise is he like that man of Resht
Whose honey none would buy in all the town.

SAHEB. What man was he?

GULBADAN. I know whom Mirza means!
Play, Dilazâr! the tune goes: "Was a maid:"

[GULBADAN *sings.*]

Was a maid sold honey-comb,
 Sweeter ran her tongue than honey;
Sweet, indeed, as sugar-reed;
 Buyers flocked to her with money:
If 't were poison she had cried,
All the town had bought and died!

One of bitter heart and face
 Marked her custom, envied her;
He 'd sell honey in her place,
 Gain the dirhams, cause the stir!

With his honey-pots he went
And his looks of ill content.

Up and down the thronged bazaar
Still he shouted, "Come and buy!"
But he found no customer,
Not so much as one blue fly.
Some one spake at evening's hour,
"Sour mouth maketh sweetness sour!"

MIRZA. Aye, girl! hearts must unchurl themselves for this!
And Sa'di truly saith, in what ensues,
There is no power in Love Love to command:

[*The* MIRZA *reads.*]

Not always Love breeds Love! Two cousins wedded,
Two sun-bright ones,—with wealth and high race steaded;
For her to call him Lord befell divinely,
For him 't was shame and shamming, since they bedded.

She showed all gentilesse and tender grace;
He to the wall turned constantly his face;

She decked herself for joy of love and living,
He asked for death rather than her embrace.

The village elders summoned him; they spake: —
"Thy heart is not towards her! let her take
Dowry and go!" He laughed: "Five score of sheep
No loss were, if deliverance those would make."

She of the Parî-eyebrows flayed her cheek
With her own nails. She cried: "How will ye speak
Of gain to me by ruin? Can I suffer
Life without Love? Cease ye from him to seek

"A hundred, or six hundred thousand head:
All shares are poor except I share his bed!" —
And, good sooth! that which bindeth hearts together
Is hearts-ease; otherwise the end is said!"

SAHEB. What end?

MIRZA. The end that Allah ordereth

For little hath Love taught unless it teach
Submission. Hear this next verse of the Ishk:

[*The* MIRZA *reads.*]

A certain man inquired of one who lay
Soul-stricken on the Mosque-floor, "Dost thou pray
For Life or Death?" He answered, "I ask nothing!
What He adjudges I accept alway."

MIRZA. Yet when it falls that each in the other finds
True shadow of the Heavenly Light, sure sound
Of Sama', Allah's music, — then, no fate
Will part those souls, nor make them two for one.
'T is Laila and Majnûn; — Laila who laughs
Before the Sultan, saying: "Lord of Lords!
If thou wouldst know how beautiful I am
Look on me through the eyes of my Majnûn!"
And Majnûn, proud and certain in his pain,
Who will not ever suffer that men deem

The desert leagues can separate their souls;
Will send no tidings to his Lady's ear,
As if he lived not always in her breast.

[*The* MIRZA *reads.*]

One to Majnûn spake: "Oh, of noblest lot!
What falleth that to Hayy thou comest not?
Thy love for Laila, peradventure, passes;
Thy fancy turns; thy heart no more is hot."

He heard, the hapless one, and, weeping, said:
"Good Sir, let go my skirt! Love is not dead!
I have the same heart, sorrowful and bleeding,
Pour not thy salt upon its wounds, still red!

"Thus to be severed is not to forget,
Nor absence fault, when Fate decreeth it."
Quoth t' other, "Ah, most faithful one and gentle!
Utter some errand on my tongue to set

"For Laila from Majnûn." He answered: "Bear
No message in my name to her most dear!
To speak as we were twain, and I not she,
Is treason;—where she is I, too, am there."

SAHEB. Why, such a lover might on moonbeams live!
And, see! how tenderly they silver now
Arjamand's Dome! How black the cypresses
Range in still ranks against the milk-white walls!
How stately soar the arrowy minarets
From yon dark garden where the Bird of Night
Trills the same love-lament a hundred times
To the hushed Rose, not tired of listening;
While crickets chirrup—as we chatter here—
With little voice which lives where Kings lie dumb!
If now we might but see Mumtaz the Queen
Pace in her Pleasaunce, strayed from Paradise
With beauty perfected—as Sa'di sings—
With eyes grown wise by what Death teaches Love,

With robes, splendid, but airy like these mists
Rolling o'er Jumna; and, beside her, him,
The King that had the lordly loving mind,
Happy, majestic! Hussein! is it true
That Shah Jahan never felt any wish
Apart from Arjamand? that, all those years,
Master of all the loveliness of Hind,
The Imperial Lover only lived for her?

MIRZA. They tell this story of Queen Arjamand:
So fair she was, so debonnair, so wise,
The heart of Shah Jahan slept in her lap:
Her mouth issued the King's decrees, her hands
Gave provinces away, and great commands.
No night but at her feet the Emperor
Laid down his cap of Lordship and his sword
To take soft counsel from her faithful lips.
Which many grudged, and most those other ones
The Afghan Lady — she that hath her grave
In the Kandhari Bagh — and Zan-i-Noor,

Grandchild of Abdurrahîm, Prince of the Blood:
"If we could turn His Majesty," said these,
"From Mumtaz, that were well wrought for the State,
Whose banner is become a Persian shift!
Mashallah! will naught dull those dazzling eyes?"
And some one whispered: "Best find newer eyes
More dazzling, killing passion with its like;
Since one love-chamber have these hearts of men,
And she who enters thrusts the other forth.
There is that slave-girl, come from Jessulmere,
A brown pearl of the Prophet's Paradise,
Wondrously fair — as none e'er saw: give word
They deck her with the garments of Mumtaz,
And hang the Queen's pearls round her throat, and
bring
The Rajpootni into the Queen's own room
When she is gone — so may my Lord the King
Be tenderly beguiled, and Mumtaz scorned."
And this the Palace Ladies swore was good.

SAHEB. Surely, 't was perilous?

MIRZA. Hazrat! the girl
Knew — for they told her — she must die, or gain
Life, and long favor, and large wealth in gold,
At moment when her veil should drop, and show
Full moonlight of her face. To reign, see you,
First in that Court, to win the eyes of him
Who ruled upon the "Peacock-throne," and stretched
Hands of command from Balkh to Himalay,
Was worth some risk, it seemed, of fierce farrash.[1]
Therefore — half willing, half constrained — she sate,
Trembling, upon the silks of Mumtaz' bed,
In vestments of the beauteous Queen, her face
Wrapped in the golden chuddur. Oh, 't is known
What fell, because a Palace maiden heard —
Listening outside the marble jâli-work —
And told it, word for word, to Arjamand.

DILAZÂR. Good Mirza! what befell?

MIRZA. The Sultan came

[1] The Executioner.

Clad in his private dress — white muslin clasped
With one great pearl, white cap and jewelled shoes —
And, throwing down his scimitar and shawl,
Spake with a gentle smile: "Light of my Life!
Once more I shut the great loud world away
And come to reign in this one realm I love,
The heart of Mumtaz!" Rose the Rajpootni,
All quaking underneath her rich disguise,
And bent full lowly to the King of Hind,
And kissed his feet; — then, let her chuddur fall,
And — lo! it was not Mumtaz there! his Queen!
But that strange, lovely, frightened girl, with throat
Heaving, eyes gleaming, hands on bosom clasped,
Who murmured: "Lord of all the world! thy slave
Waiteth thy will that she may live or die."

GULBADAN. Doubtless he drew his blade, and slew her there!

SAHEB. He was a man, 't is writ, of gravity;
Nice in his pride, terrible in his wrath,
I shudder, Mirza! for your slave-maiden.

MIRZA. Good Sir! you do not know how fair she was!
Otherwise who had ventured? On his lips
Ended even in beginning those dread words
Which leaped from royal anger. At mid rage
The charm unspeakable of that sweet slave,
The glory of the body of her bare
Melted his mounting fury! Allah makes
Sometimes a face and form to smite man's soul
With witchery of subtlest symmetry,
And she was such! That Lady of the Taj
Owned not such lustrous orbs, nor could have shown
Stature so cypress-like, such arms, such limbs,
Such eloquence of beauty, touched by fear
Into bewitching grace. Nay! and she marked
The first wrath in the Sultan's countenance
Flicker and pass as flame doth pass away
When rain falls on the sparkling of a brand:
So gently dropped upon his mind the rain
Of wonder, pity, will of gentilesse:

And, when she sank upon her face, and sobbed,
"Lord of the Age! forgive me! send me hence
Alive! I was not told how great thou art,
How terrible! how base and bold my deed!"
He raised the Rajpoot girl, gazed on her face
With softening eyes, and, while her heart beat quick,
Touched—with strange tremble of his hands—her hair,
Her brows, her ears: then, conquering himself,
Spake: "Get thee hence alive! Fairest thou art
Of Allah's works; and I—I am a man,
Albeit Lord of men and Shah Jahan;
Yet one thing fairer is than even thou,
And sweeter far for me to have and keep,
The faith I held and hold to her whose name
Thou art not meet to hear! Rajpootni! see,
I close mine eyes, not longer to behold
Thy beauty, lest it tempt my rebel blood
To traitorousness like thine. Begone! begone!

Before I look again; for I shall slay,
Or I shall love, and both were deeds indign!"

SAHEB. Right royal! and nowise of the Mogul type,
As I have read. What next befell that slave,
With respite of eye-wink?

MIRZA. She glided forth,
Seeking escape; but those that heard the words
And saw all done, laid hands on her and haled
The weeping maid to angry Arjamand,
Decked as she was in the Queen's cloth of gold,
Wearing the Palace-pearls, ungirt, new-bathed,
Painted, and henna-stained, and scented sweet.
They told what passed, and how the Sultan spake,
She cowering at the proud Sultana's foot.

DILAZÂR. Then the Queen stabbed her to the heart—was 't not?
Straight to the heart! Wallah! I would have stabbed!

MIRZA. Then the Queen drew the dagger from her waist,
A knife of watered steel, hafted with jade,

And on the hilt a ruby worth three lakhs,
Pigeon-blood color, marvellous, the gift
Of Shah Jahan in some soft hour of love —
An unmatched stone. And, when they looked to see
The keen point pierce the panting satin skin
Stripped of its veil — Arjamand stooped and placed
The dagger-blade beneath her sandal, snapped
The bright steel short, and, drawing near to hers
That Rajpoot's face, kissed tenderly her mouth,
And gravely spake: "Go! thou hast given me
The richest, best, last gift which Earth could give
In comfort of my great Lord's constancy.
Take thou this jewel of my dagger, Friend! —
Nowise its point! — and a Queen's thanks therewith
For treason dearly done to Arjamand!"

So passed the Rajpoot, rich and scatheless, thence.

SAHEB. Sweeter her memory seems for that one deed
Of loftiest clemency than for her face

Of heavenly charm, or for her sovereignties,
Or fame or tomb! How think you, Gulbadan?

GULBADAN. My Lord! I marvel, and admire! but this
Is like strange golden fruit grown on tall trees
In other gardens than where Nautchnees live!
They will not think we have the right to love
Such lovely things and thoughts. They do not give
Even a heart to us whose portion is
To sing, and dance, and be desirable,
For daily bread. Ask Mirza Hussein else!
The Mohsinât, the women who are wed,
The proud and happy ones with faces veiled,
For them, born on the lap of Rectitude,
Is comfort here, and after — Paradise;
But for us contumely and after — Hell.
I know it, for the Mollah read to me
Sura the Twenty-Fourth, intituled "Light,"
And therefore 't is not meet you ask of us

If Arjamand wrought well: only I feel
One might do queenly deeds, nurtured a queen.

DILAZÂR. Will the Saheb think none but a queen doth such?
I knew a singing-girl with soul as large
As Arjamand's, if I might tell of it.

SAHEB. Calamity of hearts! If Hussein please,
Recite your story.

DILAZÂR. Oh, my Lord! 't is brief!
We journeyed with a company to play
Two rains ago; and she I tell you of,
Our chiefest singer, took the road with us;
A Bird of Women — pleasant, patient, bright,
With eyes our hard lives never once made bold:
A common girl I say — born to the bells,
But gentle, winsome, so that wayfarers,
Seeing her face, would cry: "God go your Friend!"
"Khudâwand Hâfiz! Sister, with the smile!"
And shy things of the jungle and the grove

Had never dread of her — crows, mynas, doves —
But perked and pecked, close to her feet, unfeared.
So fell it that we rested on our path,
Eating and drinking by a forest-pool;
And hard by camped some Brahmans, pilgriming
To Muttra, women, children, householders,
Rich folk and proud. But while we tarried there —
Those high-caste people holding far aloof
From taint of us — one small brown baba left
Its mother's breast, a little naked maid
Two years of age, maybe: wilful she crept
Across the sand, and found our Singing-girl,
And nestled to her heart, cooing soft sounds,
And winding in between her arms, the way
Young birds have when they reach the wings they love.
You are too great to know or care for this,
But women melt to touch of baby hands,
And she was fondling, lulling this soft friend
Who knew the sweetness of her soul as bees

Know where the honey hides in jungle-flowers,
When near at hand, the angry mother spied,
And ran, and snatched her babe away, and screamed:
"Poison it not, thou woman of bazaars!
With thine accursèd lips and arms for hire;
Give me my babe, and get thee to thy trade,
Which hath no good, nor grace of children's love!"
And we were wroth and would have fallen on them;
But she, the Mild-faced, laughed, and said, "Let be!
The Brahman mother hath much right to scorn!"

GULBADAN. Sister! I cannot think the Presences
Will care to hear.

SAHEB. Now, Gulbadan, be still!
If you are weary, sleep!

DILAZÂR. They took the road;
And afterwards we followed, when the Sun
Made longer shadows. At a lonely spot
Where Imri trees grew round a tank, thick-set
With rocks, and one white Temple by the tank—

Ill-named for savage beasts, a place of fear —
We hear loud cries. The Brahman father runs
Shouting to those with us, "Ah, Friends! your spears!
Your tulwars! Shiva, Shiva! help us, help!"
Then, when his breath was fetched, the good man told —
Sorely lamenting — how his wife had laid
Her sleeping baby in that Temple-yard
While at the tank they bathed; and how, half-washed,
They marked a great gaunt Tigress from the wood
Stalk forth, and sniff the Temple-steps, and pass
Into the Temple-court; and there she couched
Watching the infant yet asleep, if yet
It slept in that most dreadful company,
Since none could see or know; nay, all were fled
For life's sake; only, in a peepul tree,
Hard by the shrine, a camel-man had climbed
And he was calling "Haste! if ye would aid!
The beast is not yet hungered, and she plays,
Licking her jowls, curling her tail: she lies

Eying the babe, which doth not move! oh, haste!"

SAHEB. Note, Gulbadan! how well this tale is told:
Why should you draw your sari o'er your face?
Are you not trembling for the pretty maid?
Would God I had been there, rifle in hand!

DILAZÂR. That had been death, Protector of the Poor!
To the sleeping child. At any show of arms
The beast had leaped upon the prey it watched
Across that Temple-court. There was one hope —
To come between the Tigress and the child
Before its mood changed, while it surmised still
Some trap, some mischief in its sleeping food —
This we knew, and the Singing-girl, and all;
But how to come?

GULBADAN: Why will you still go on,
Dear Dilazâr?

MIRZA. The peril frightens her;
It troubles me!

SAHEB. Nay! but the way to save
That helpless child? I cannot find a way!

DILAZÂR. This common woman could! I heard her say,
"The baby is my baby of the morn
Who wound its arms about my neck, and kissed
My mouth with innocent lips! See! I will go
And take my friend forth from the Tiger's mouth,
If God shall please! And if He shall not please
Why, 't is a Singing-girl the brute will eat,
And not that tender one, born to live pure!"
So, ere a hand could stay her, she had drawn
The sari tight between her knees, and walked,
With those kind eyes fixed hard upon the beast,
Straight to the spot — had stooped — had gathered close
The silent child against that heart which beat
Fearless of fear — had reached the steps again,
Steadfastly eying always those fierce eyes
That glared and sparkled, blazing rage and dread;
Her face always full-turned to that fell face

Cushioned upon spread paws, yet stirring not;
For, Sirs! as God is God, the love of it,
The greatness of it, and the suddenness —
Which, as I do perceive, hold now your minds —
Lay on that snarling, bristling beast of blood,
A spell and wonder which it could not burst
For all the savage pantings of its strength:
And she had gained the porch, the outer steps,
Ere, with a roar as when the thunder cracks
A black-bound cloud, mad to be free and safe
From the sweet terror of those mastering eyes,
The Tigress bounded through the air — a flash
Of living lightning — passed the porch, one claw
Striking the girl, tearing her choli down,
But oh! a skin-wound only! for the beast
Sought quick escape; and safe she came to us
Clasping the babe, red with her gentle blood;
And so the mother took her infant back
A gift from the Bazaar-girl!

SAHEB. Gulbadan —

As we may judge from her averted head —

Hardly believes you!

DILAZÂR. Well! she doubts herself

If she doubts that bold deed. Look, Sirs! I turn

The choli from her shoulder! there 's the seal

The Tigress stamped upon it — for 't was she!

[*Both the men rise, and make salutation to* GULBADAN.]

MIRZA. *Afrin!* O Girl! an old man honors thee!

While I have thought to play the teacher here,

Reciting Ishk, and all our Sûfic lore,

And how men pass from low to high, and learn

From Love to conquer love of self, and come

Nearer to Him, the Friend, who is Love's self,

Here is a Singing-girl turns my last page

And teacheth Sa'di! Gulbadan! Salaam!

SAHEB. Dear Gulbadan! brave, loving Gulbadan!

Salaam! if Agra only owns the thing,
Or has a sonar working worthily,
You shall have such an armlet for that arm —
Which bears its red wound like a Rose of God —
Of tiger-claws set in fine gold, to make
The whole gay taïfah envious of you!
Is 't true? did those eyes stare a Tigress down?
Did that brown satin wrist and little hand
Forbid the man-eater her bloody meal?

GULBADAN. I did it, Saheb! for the baby's sake
Who loved me so, unasked. It was not hard!
I was afraid — the beast was more afraid!
It would have leaped, but had not time to think.

SAHEB. I think, if Arjamand and Shah Jahan
Walked in their Garden — as we said — to-night,
The Queen would give another such a gem
As that great ruby of the hilt, to you!
And if the Sultan heard this Ishk with us,
I think that he would say, "Where in my Hind

Is he had done for manhood and for me —
Though he knew Sa'di as wise Hussein knows —
What for a baby's kiss your Singing-girl
Did and forgot, till Dilazâr's light tongue
Fetched the sweet truth forth, as the honey-bird
Pecks nectar from the tight-shut trumpet flower?"
Right-learnèd Friend! is not this also Love
As true as Majnûn's?

MIRZA. Yea, Sir! Love to praise!
To ponder, worship, wonder at, and thank —
By the perspicuous Book! — for nobleness
Which yields us high example, and makes plain
Life is a little gift when Love bids "give!"

DILAZÂR. Oh, Sister! hanging down your head for shame
Like yonder rose heavy with early dew,
To hear these Presences! Now is your face
Made white, shy Rose! but I — if I have leave —
Will be your Bulbul, since there comes to mind
A little song Lord Sa'di made for this.

[DILAZÂR *sings.*]

A Drop of Rain was falling from forth a summer cloud,
It saw the ocean under it roll billows large and loud;
And, all-ashamed and sore-dismayed, it whispered "Woe is me!
By Allah! I am naught! what counts one Rain-drop to the Sea?"

But while it mocked and mourned itself—for littleness forlorn—
Into a sea-shell's opened lips the Drop of Rain was borne,
Where many a day and night it lay, until at last it grew
A lovely Pearl of lucent ray, faultless in form and hue;

And God our Lord, who knoweth best how sea-fish make His gem,
Caused those that dive to bring it up;—so in the diadem
Of Persia's King they set that Pearl, and so the Rain-drop came
To be a Sultan's pride and wealth, a Jewel of great name!

In that it fell, for loftiness that Rain-drop was designed;
It rose to majesty and worth, because of modest mind!
O Sa'di! here thou singest sooth! Who waits at Door of Fate
With lowly heart and humble voice finds unexpected state.

MIRZA. True, Friends! it is not station, birth, nor wealth,
Nor power, nor learning lends us grace to grow
A Pearl upon the Neck-string of the Friend!
And this next lesson will the Ishk impart:

[*The* MIRZA *reads.*]

They mocked the Sovereign of Ghaznin: one saith,
"Ayaz hath no great beauty, by my faith!
A Rose that's neither rosy-red nor fragrant,
The Bulbul's love for such astonisheth!"

This went to Mahmud's ears; ill-pleased he sate,
Bowed on himself, reflecting: then to that
Replied: "My love is for his kindly nature,
Not for his stature, nor his face, nor state!"

And I did hear how, in a rocky dell,
Bursting a chest of gems a camel fell:
King Mahmud waved his sleeve, permitting plunder,
But spurred his own steed onward, as they tell.

His horsemen parted from their Lord amain,
Eager for pearls, and corals, and such gain:
Of all those neck-exalting courtiers
None except Ayaz near him did remain.

The King looked back—"How many hast thou won,
Curled comfort of my heart?" He answered "None!
I galloped up the pass in rear of thee;
I quit thee for no pearls beneath the sun!"

Oh, if to God thou hast propinquity,
For no wealth heedless of His service be!
If Lovers true of God shall ask from God
Aught except God, that's infidelity!

If thine eyes fix on any gift of Friend
Thy gain, not his, is thy desire's end!
If thy mouth gape in avarice, Heaven's message
Unto Heart's ear by that road shall not wend!

SAHEB. I see it is not willed that Love should gain,
Nor pay itself with pleasure, nor sit soft
On this world's carpets, drinking wine of ease.
But, all in drawing closer to the "Friend"
(Your Sûfic word) — the Cup-bearer — forego
Those passing pearls and corals of Life's chance,
The plunder of the camel's broken chest,
For glory of far greater joys, for bliss
Of sacrifice, for ecstasy of death

Which buys for the Belovèd life, for meed
To hear the Sultan of all Sultans say,
"Curled Darling of my heart!" as He shall say
To those who rode near to His Flag of Love
All through Earth's gloomy pass, unwavering,
Disdaining profit. Learnèd Mirza! so
Your Ishk comes, by its Persian road of palms
And nightingales, and roses, and soft verse,
To that same Syrian Hill whose slopes austere
Heard our Lord Isa speak: "*I say to you*
Love ye your enemies! Be in your love
Perfect, as is your Father Who is Love!
Take no thought for your life: the Kingdom first!
God's Kingdom first! God's righteousness! and then
Other things shall be added!" And, it comes —
Your Sûfic Ishk, with "Cup" and "Cup-bearer,"
Down all these garden-paths — to that green tree
Whereunder sate my Buddha, when he taught
Ahinsa, and the Law of Love and Peace,

The "Noble Truths" and high Nirvâna's word.
Only, I find not that your Prophet prized
This doctrine of the all-embracing Love,
Gentle to enemies, submissive, sweet,
Foregoing, and forgiving: seeking bliss
In gift, and gain by loss, contemning self,
Heedless of safety in the lust to save,
Like our good Gulbadan, who from that beast
Redeemed imperiously the babe she loved,
Terrible in her tenderness of heart,
Stronger than death — all by Love's sorcery,
The *Jadoo* of your Ishk!

MIRZA. Allah assoil
The boldness of thy tongue, dear Friend! there lacks
Nothing hereof to the Perspicuous Book:
But when our Lord (on whom be peace!) received
Jibrâil's message, 't was to his own race —
The lean, fierce, desert-seasoned Bedaween —
This came; and it was very meet God's word

Should fall in thunder on their ears, not songs;
Should scourge to rightfulness with Hell's khamseen,
Not lure them thither with sweet airs of Heaven.
And, for the rest, our holy Koran saith:
"Allah hath given to every land its Book,
Its Prophet to each people."

SAHEB. Ah! your Hell—
Al-Zakkum's ghastly fruit! the "Shoes of flame"!
Al Hotama, where sinful Christians roast!
How fits th' Eternal Love, the "Friend," with those?

MIRZA. *Toba!* Saheb, *toba!* Ibn-us-Sammak spake
The master-word hereon: "Fear God, O Man!
As though not once thou hadst obeyed His word;
And trust the Love of God, O Man! as though
Thou never once hadst disobeyed His laws!"

SAHEB. But why make bloody tigers and sly snakes?
The evil things and ugly of this Earth?
What place have such, if all is God and Love?

MIRZA. Tigers are not so murderous as men

Arrayed in battle, or by hate inflamed;
Nor snakes as sly and deadly. For ill-looks
Each to his kind shows fair. We have heard here
Your Mollahs of the West hold Adam's sons
Sprung of the Sea-slug, and, by apish sires,
Down through slow shapings of the bone and brain,
Developed from the savage to the sage;
So might you, surely, with more patience wait
Fixed working-out of steadfast primal plans
In beast and serpent, poison-bag and fang!
For us it is enough that Allah's will
Found them their place and purpose in His World;
And 't is of this the Ishk now witnesseth:

[*The* MIRZA *reads.*]

Philosophy goes many a winding road,
Now here she turns — now there — on ways re-trod;
For Lovers of the Friend straight leads the pathway,
They see and know and seek nothing save God!

This is a plain thing unto all with eyes,
But Doctors of Dispute hold otherwise:
"The Sky and Earth," they ask, "the sons of Adam,
Birds, Beasts, and Snakes, how wilt thou such comprise?"

Yea! Ahl-i-Kiyâs! learnèd masters, yea!
'Tis an approvèd knot this which ye say:
If answer be permitted, Sa'di answers,
"He is in all things, and by Him are they;

"The plains, the seas, the mountain, and the mist,
Men, Pâris, Angels, Jinns — all that subsist,
All, whatsoever is, lives comprehended;
Only by His existing these exist.

"Huge rolls the sea — we know — in foam and spray
Under our feet, with dreadful waves at play;
Bright climbs to topmost of the firmament
The broad and blinding Sun, Sultan of Day.

" Yet, if ye deem them something outside Him,
Then are ye ' Peoples of the Picture!' Dim
Your lamps gleam! never will ye find a passage
To that far other Land where Seraphim

" And Lords of Truth sit saying: 'Yon gold Sun,
It is not of His smallest treasures one!
Yon Ocean, seven times folded, if He willed it,
Exhales, like dew-drop in the noon undone!'

" Oh, when the Sultan of all State appears,
And Royal Banner of the real Life rears,
This world into the neck of Non-existence
Draws head, as when a tortoise footsteps fears!"

MIRZA. And this our Lord will still exemplify.

[*The* MIRZA *reads.*]

The Raïs of a village, with his son,
Encountered on a certain road alone,

The main-guard of a monarch's army marching,
A myriad pacing with the step of one.

Marvelling the boy beheld the pioneers,
With swords and battle-axes; halberdiers,
Heralds and scouters; glistering shirts of satin,
Waist-cloths of gold, horse-trappings, shields and spears;

Ranks of fierce fighting-men, bearing the bow;
And after them those that with quivers go
Furnishing shafts; a blaze of bright silk yonder,
And here a King's cap in the glorious show:

Which pomp and splendor watching—when he turned
To speak the joy wherewith his young blood burned,
Lo! the exceeding meanness of his Father!
At that loud storm of war sorely concerned

The old man's mien was changed, his color fled,
His heart made water; and, with fear half-dead,

Into a cave he hied. The Son inquired,
"Art thou not Raïs, as the folks have said?

"Chief of our Tribe, and by such chieftaincy
Named with the great ones? What hath come to thee,
To snap the staff of manhood, and with terror
To tremble like a wind-torn willow-tree?"

The Sire replied: "Yea! truly I am chief,
And of the great — at home; but this belief
Goeth not past our village!" —
Even likewise
The mightiest are o'erwhelmed with awe and grief

Who come upon the march of God the King.
Oh, thou of mortal sort! why should it bring
Pride to thy soul to rule in this world's village?
Thy state and greatness is a little thing!

SAHEB. Truly a little thing! See where we sit
In this fair Garden with its milk-white Tomb
Gleaming behind the palms, and those great Dead
Whose joy it was, who ruled the spacious land,
Lie out of sight under two narrow slabs,
Forgot, unseen — the Sultan and his Love —
Arjamand Banu Begam, Shah Jahan,
Two basketsful of dust and crumbled bones!

MIRZA. Yes, that hath solemness, if we did look
Not farther than to trivial circumstance
Of death, and dust, and darkness of the grave;
And common is the homily thereon;
Even Sa'di hath this skull-verse I recall:

[*The* MIRZA *recites.*]

Say not Sultans are mighty! think not largely of thrones!
The realm of the beggar is safer than the kingdoms of diademed ones:

The lighter the wallet is loaded the farther the traveller
goes;
And the crown is a heavier headgear than felt, as a
Darweesh knows.

The woe of a Darweesh is measured by his want of an
oaten crust;
On the heart of a King sit always his Empire's toil and
trust.

When the Darweesh has munched at sunset his hunk
of yesterday's bread,
He sleeps in his rags more sweetly than the King on a
golden bed.

Be grieved for whoso ruleth, and pity his sorrowful fate!
The beggar is verily monarch, though he hides with
a clout his state.

I heard it told of a Darweesh, long ago, in a distant
land,
How a skull spake these words to him, as he held the
thing in his hand:

"The pomp of the giving of orders, and the power to
save and to slay,
Were mine; and a turban of greatness on the brow
which is bone to-day.

"God's will and the glory of battle brought harvest to
edge of my sword;
I was King of the two great Rivers, I was Babylonia's
Lord:

"I had in my heart the purpose to seize Karamania's
plain!—
When lo!—in the wink of an eyelid—the worms
were eating my brain!"—

From the Ear of Wisdom, Darweesh! the Cotton of
Carelessness pluck,
That counsel of dead men, Darweesh! may bring thee,
by lowliness, luck.

SAHEB. Your own glad Poet, then, touched strings so
sad?

MIRZA. Sir! he wrote thus. But whoso deems life
ends
With what a skull saith, and the wormy talk
Of mortal minutes finished, wotteth not
Of inner times unfolding, and large days
Beyond our dawns, and Beauty beautified
Past Arjamand, past Laila and Majnûn.
They who take hopelessness for truth, and sit
On carpet of Resignment, looking not
Except for Death to undo Life's slow-wove web,
Ravelling the pattern — toilsome, finished, rich —
Just when God's shuttle shot the last thread home,
Are like those apes which caught a fire-fly
And laid it 'neath green sticks, and blew, and blew,
Hoping to kindle light. See there! 't is full —
Yon cypress-top, the Tree of gloom — with sparks
Born of the swamp and the wan water! Look!
Should one take those pale fluttering specks for stars?
And hear how Sa'di mocketh them! he saith:

[*The* MIRZA *reads.*]

In mead or grove, by night, oft hast thou seen
The fire-fly wave his lamp of glittering green:
Once some one said, "Oh, Fly! lamping the darkness,
What makes it that thy kind hath never been

"Spied in the day-time?" Mark what answer wise
That little marsh-born thing, with fiery eyes,
Gave from its mouth of luminosity!—
"Wherever waters spread, and dank leaves rise,

"We range, day-time and night-time; but the Sun
Puts out our gleam: till his great race is run
Our feeble beams are nowhere manifest;
The darkness kindles them, when night's begun!"

SAHEB. Yet, Mirza! men will press that Death is Death,
Painful and hateful, ending tender Love;

That Beauty, like the rose, drops her sweet leaves,
And eyes of youth, which saw Heaven's smile therein,
Grow dim and hopeless; and ten thousand ills
Palsy the heart's wings mounting hopefullest:
Till, at the last — whether we pile on it
A mountain of snow-marble, like this Taj,
Or clay on clay — here lies the sum of all
Arjamand, dead in child-bed, dust and bones!
Her Sultan, crownless, fleshless, good to make
Pipkins for potters! Ah, the bitterness!

MIRZA. What "bitterness"? What "sum"? Did men complain,
Waiting so long and still in the safe womb,
Before the Maker's scheme gave them glad birth
And resurrection into present life,
With roses, and delights, and lips and songs,
So dear to have you cannot brook to lose?
Oh, Allah! pardon men, who are as babes
That will not open hands to clasp Thy hand

Lest they unclasp the play-things given them
To make the sunlight sweet 'twixt sleep and sleep!
Listen once more to Sa'di, teaching peace:

[*The* MIRZA *reads.*]

A tumult in a Syrian town had place;
They seized an old man there of wit and grace;
Still in my ear lingers his noble saying,
When, fettered fast, they smote him on the face:

Quotha: "If of all Sultans the Sultân
Gives not the word for plunder, who else can?
Who, save upon His bidding, would be bold
To do such deeds? Therefore I hold the man,

"That wrongs me, not mine enemy but friend;
God hath appointed him unto this end!
If there fall scorn or honor, gifts or shackles,
'Tis God—not Zayd or Omar—who doth send."—

Right, Sheykh! no griefs the wise heart will annoy;
The Great Physician sharp drugs doth employ!
A sick man's not more skilful than his Hâkim;
Take what the Friend gives as a bliss and joy.

SAHEB. Good! if we knew, as this calm ancient knew,
All things from Him!
MIRZA. How were it otherwise?
Or, have you thought the stars and worlds are left,
The angels, and the jinns, and men — those least
Last creatures of the Universe, yet lodged
In palace of this wondrous Earth, roofed o'er
With sapphire, and with emerald pavemented —
To Shaitan, to Azâzil? If the worm
Will wrap itself in self-made shroud of silk,
Glad to quit being, sure of life to come,
Trusting the secret promise of the hours
To bring it wings of cream and gold, and feasts
Of blossoms brimmed with honey; if she-bears

Have love enough for their shagged cubs to dash
Careless upon the spear-blade — shall not we
Have sense and grace to wait for Him to give
Who giveth all, to trust the Cup-bearer
Whatever wine He pour?

DILAZÂR. Most learnèd one!
Is it taught true that, when Believers die,
The spirits of them dwell in green birds' crops
Under the Throne, until the Trumpet blows?

MIRZA. The birds are milk-white, Daughter! Yet who knows
Of *Al-Berzakh*, and of the bone *Al Ajb*
Wherefrom all spring anew? Have thou in mind
How when our Lord the Prophet (on his tomb
Shine Allah's light!) questioned Jibrâil's self
Of this, and of the "Blast of Summoning,"
The holy Angel answered, "Times and signs
We wot not! Allah wotteth!" And, hear now
What Sa'di saith of God's sufficiency:

[*The* MIRZA *reads.*]

A Prince praised Saïd, Zangi's Son: quoth he,
"Much mercy on his tomb-stone may there be!
Dirhams I gave him, and a dress of honor,
And kept for him a seat of dignity.

" But on my robe of honor when he read
'Allah wa bas' *writ large in golden thread,*
With sudden heat he plucked that garment from him,
And such flame caught his spirit that he fled

" Into the waste. One of the Desert-breed
Asked, 'Saïd, Son of Zangi! what didst read
Worked on the khillat, that, in act to worship
Thou shouldst, with rude heel, on the good gift tread?'

" He laughed and answered: 'I was over-fraught
With pride at first; but when I saw that wrought

"GOD IS ENOUGH!" *upon the gilded silk,*
I did remember all the rest was naught.'"

SAHEB. Noble thy scroll is, Mirza! strange to muse
This Sa'di fought our soldiers of the Cross
In old days for the Holy Sepulchre,
At Askalon, and Lebanon! How mad
Are nations' quarrels! righteous work, forsooth,
For Heaven and Christ that Red-Cross Knight had
wrought,
Who should have cloven brain with such rhymes rich,
Or driven blundering consecrated lance
Through such a Paynim's heart.

MIRZA. Doubt thou not, Sir!
He battled, as he teacheth, valiantly:
'T is told he thrice set free a Nazarene —
Unhorsed, and helpless at his dagger's point —
Ere he was made a slave at Tripoli.

[GULBADAN *starts and cries aloud:*]

GULBADAN. *Ya Ali!* help me, help!

SAHEB. What is it?

MIRZA. Girl!

Khûda bad na dihad! [1] What aileth?

GULBADAN. Oh!

I thought a scorpion crept beneath my cloth!

Some winged thing 'twas flew in my neck: 'tis naught!

Pardon me, Sirs!

SAHEB. Our sweet-voiced Gulbadan,

Who did not dread the tiger's blazing eyes,

Screams at a moth! When shall we ever learn

This book of man?

MIRZA. It came for love of flame

Into the burning lamp: nay, Dilazâr!

Kill it not! 'tis a creature, too, of God,

And flutters towards the light, like us: I mind

A little ghazal which doth bid thee spare:

[1] God send thee no evil.

[*The* MIRZA *recites.*]

Who is so small but, when he suffers, sighs?
Who is so great but mercy dignifies?

Shibli, from grain bazaar, upon his back
With toilsome steps took home a loaded sack;

Arrived — a red Ant in the wheat he spied,
Her troubled feet running from side to side.

"I to my house, and thou to thine!" quoth he;
"Testify at the Judgment this of me!"

For pity of her woe all that long way,
He bore her to her people of the clay:

And Firdausi this gentle verse did make,
"Peace be to his pure Tomb for that Ant's sake!"

DILAZÂR. Sir! I have sent it free, the spotted moth!
If I sate many nights in your Bostàn

I think I should grow good and wise; but look!
The Wolf's Tail sweeps the sky, soon 't will be dawn!

MIRZA. Yes, we must finish! And the fluttering moth
Is Sa'di's image now of Love which lives
Faithful unto the end in trust of Love:

[*The* MIRZA *reads.*]

Hear what the little soft-winged Moth replied,
Fluttering around the lamp-flame, ere he died,
To one who said: "Creature contemptible!
Some Mistress choose to thine own kind allied,

"Some road of Love, which holds forth hope, pursue,
Thou and thy Wick's embraces! What's to do
Betwixt ye? Whence and whither such mad passion?
Burnest thou? Ay! and candle burneth, too!

"Thou art not a Samundar to pass free
Mid scorching coals; let the hot lantern be!
Since Sense comes first, and after Sacrifice;
And blind bats leave the Sun to such as see.

"Vainly against a stronger force we strive;
And foolish 't is in gentilesse to live
With those declared our enemies! Who taught thee
'Twas right thy being for her beams to give?

"Hast thou not heard how, once, a Beggar wooed
The daughter of a King, and boldly sued
To wed her; and the pushings on his neck
How hard they were; the blows how sore and rude?

"A lover like to thee why should she bring
Into heart's count, when Agha, Mirza, King
Turn their great faces towards her for their light?
In such high company think no vain thing

"That she can show thee tenderness! Good lack!
Tender she might be to the general pack,
But thou art of the helpless ones! thy softness
With scorn consuming she will pay thee back."

Listen what answer made the ardent Moth:—
"No matter if I burn, oh, thou too wroth!
Such fire is in my breast, like Ibrahim's,
That flames become Rose-gardens to us both!

"My hand draws not my Lady's skirts, I know!
But she draws me! And yet, it is not so:
Strong love for her this is which claims and draws me;
It is not wholly of my will I go

"To win red Kiss of Death. Afar, afar
I was as burnt as now my poor wings are
Here, in the flame. The worst of fire befell me
Then, when my love first kindled at her Star."

SAHEB. You see it was for comfort that he fled,
Rose-Body! to your neck! How could he dream,
Kind Gulbadan, brave Gulbadan, who takes
Their prey from tigers, would have feared a moth?

GULBADAN. Ah, Treasure-house of Bounty! I am shamed!
I did not know this was so sad a one.
Read, Mirza Saheb! what the Moth said next.

MIRZA. Still went he on, exalting constancy:

[*The* MIRZA *reads.*]

" Yet, in regard of Beauty no men pray
For less of Beauty — tho' that Beauty slay!
Who then reproves me, loving my Belovèd,
Since Life at her white feet well-pleased I lay?

" Dost thou not know why I court doom and Death?
That she may live when I have yielded breath!

For that is fit! and she, my Best belovèd
Burns brightlier when my flesh enkindleth.

" *How wilt thou say, then, 'Find thyself some mate*
Suitable, equal, more compassionate'?
'Tis all as though to one by scorpion bitten
Thou shouldst cry 'Grieve not!' as console my state.

" *Idle is counsel which men cannot take,*
And vain to urge, when one his reins doth break,
'Ay, Gholam! drive thou slower!' 'Twas well written,
Ishk atesh ast; *and wind worse fire doth make!*

" *Advice is wind, and passion is as flame;*
The panther by his wounds fiercer became:
Thou art dull-witted, being what thou seemest,
To deem that I, a Lover, am the same.

"Let worshippers of Self seek such as they,
In spots secure, and by an easy way;
Those drunk with heavenly self-forgetfulness
Go on a perilous quest, glad if it slay.

"When first with this desire I grew possessed,
All other hopes I rooted from my breast;
He that will stake his head is called true Lover;
The feeble-livered loves his life the best.

"What? on a sudden, from some ambush, Death
Ends me in some vile way? Better my breath
To yield as I will yield it, willing-minded,
Doomed by my Lady's swift delicious wrath!

"'Tis written on the brow when we must die;
If she's to kill, 'Right welcome!' answer I;
Since one day, helpless, we must quit existence,
Now at her feet I lay it, joyously!"

GULBADAN. If there were lovers like to him 'mongst men,
Women would be, as breeze of Mosellay
Gentle and steadfast; and, as Ruknabad,[1]
Limpid and sweet!

DILAZÂR. Yet I am fain to hear
What spake the lamp!

MIRZA. It answereth in the next:

[*The* MIRZA *reads.*]

One night—I do remember—when mine eyes
Closed not, I heard a talking in this wise:
Moth said to Lamp-flame, "Ah, my Well-belovèd!
I am a Lover; this is no surprise

"If I do weep and burn; but thou! but thou!
Why do I see thee weeping, burning, now?"
The Lamp replied, "Shirîn-i-man! *Soft Lover!*
The honey of my life melts from my brow!"

[1] A spot and stream mentioned by Hafiz.

It said, " Oh, tearful Lover! cease to sigh!
Passion's worst pangs thou knowest not, as I:
Leave claiming, leave lamenting, or come boldly!
Nor power, nor patience of Love's mystery

" Hast thou, who fliest from my naked fire,
Desiring, yet afraid of thy Desire!
Hither and thither dost thou flutter, fearful;
But I consume, exhale, glow and expire.

" If flame of Love thy silver feathers scorch,
Look upon me, who am Love's kindled Torch!
Think on the blaze and torrent of my burning,
Forget my splendor, lighting Court and Porch!"

There lingered still some little of the night,
When one of Pâri-face put out that light;
The smoke rose like a parting soul: it whispered,
" Look, Lover! now, indeed, Love endeth right!

"*This is the Road!* Rah in ast! *learn of me;*
Dying thou gainest Love's best ecstasy!"

. . . .

Make over Lover slain no lamentation;
Cry Shukur! *thanks!—He is accepted; he.*

Oh, if thou be'st true Lover wash not hand
From that dear stain of Love! from worldly brand
Of wealth and self-love wash it! At the last
Those win, who spite of Fortune's tempests, stand,

Glad to wreck all for Love. I say to thee—
I, Sa'di—launch not on that boundless Sea!
But, if thou puttest forth, hoist sail, quit anchor!
To storm and wave trust thyself hardily!

SAHEB. I think, with Dilazâr, if we should sit
Ofttimes, good Mirza! in Bostân with you,
We might almost grow bold as Gulbadan
For Allah's holy sake, and what He made;

Might learn to love like Candle and like Moth.
And, of a truth, by this we may perceive
Whither your Poet brings us. But now dance
One little measure more, and sing that song
The Nautchnees use at parting, Gulbadan!
Then will I tell you what our Hindoos say —
The pundits of the Poorans and the Ved —
Touching this Love in Life, and all it means.

GULBADAN. Janâb! I think it is this dance you ask,
Where first we lay aside chuddur and veil
And glide near to the Feast-master, and gaze
Eyes into eyes; and then again put on
The garments, and steal slow away, and hide
Our face, the music softly dying down:

[*She dances and sings;* DILAZÂR *playing.*]

I have danced, oh, my Master and Lover!
All my best;

It is past, I shall no more discover
Neck and breast!
Thou hast seen, thou hast seen! and, by glances
Deep impressed —
The beat of my feet in the dances
Told the rest.

Jan-i-man! Life of mine, it is ended!
O'er my face
I draw veil! Music no more is blended
In this place
With the songs where Love's sigh comprehended
Soul's embrace:
Khûda Hâfiz! God keep you attended
By His grace!

SAHEB. Thanks, most kind Gulbadan! Tulip and Bird!
Dancer and Singer both, and both so sweet!
Yes! it is this the Sânkhya maxim taught
In *Nartakiva*[1] (do you know it, Sir?),
Saying ('t is section sixty-nine, book three

[1] Nartakivatpravittasyâpi nivrittischaritârthyât, &c., &c.

Of Kapila) in Sanskrit terse and dark:
"For Nature, in the shows and plays of life,
Is like a dancing-girl who paces, sings,
Reveals, conceals, approaches, and retires
Before the eyes of him whom she would move;"
Till — when it is enough — she drops her veil,
And speaks the word of rest, and ceases so,
(As Gulbadan did, when tamboora stayed),
And then an end for him; since Soul is taught.

GULBADAN. Ah, English Lord! but those that teach the Soul,
Obeying Nature, or hard need, or fate;
Or set to this by whatso force or fault;
Have you no happy wisdom, too, for us?

SAHEB. My Tiger-tamer! with the roe-deer eyes,
What should I know? Heaven hath its scheme for you,
Its pity, and its pardon, and its love,
Even as for queens. Nature doth dance for you
As for her best; matches her songs to ear,

Makes eye-play, heart-play, till she fill your soul
With what was meant. *Inshallah!* be well-pleased!
Would I had such good hope as Gulbadan!

DILAZÂR. But what *is* meant? Huzoor! for these high words
Make even Nautchnees muse.

SAHEB. Calamity
Of heedless minds, bright Dilazâr! 't were best
If Hussein answered, for the Mirza's wit
Guides us herein — yet we three witless ones
Glean thus much, as I deem, from this fair night
Spent in the Garden of Queen Arjamand:
That all the glory and the grace of things,
Witchcraft of loveliness, wonder of flesh,
Fair symmetry of forms, deep harmonies
Of line and limb — are but as shadows cast
From hidden Light of Beauty and of Love
Thus chiefly here revealed. Nor charm alone
Of man for woman, woman for the man,

With secret of Earth's roll kept thus at speed,
And all its tender fruits of motherhood,
And fatherhood, and friendships, and large links
Of households, villages, towns, nations, race;
But all things beautiful and great which please,
Those wonder-whispering stars, that poised swift moon,
The purple peace of Night, yon pearly Dawn
Colored with day's first gold; this cool pure breeze
Which is the breath of Nature wakening,
Those roses with their lovely blush come back,
These birds withdrawing little heads from wings,
The butterflies abroad spreading soft vans
Of blue and green and crimson, silver-mealed;
The blossoms opening for them, honey-filled,
And stately things and rich of Art, where Man
Works to the patterns of the Master-hand,
Such as yon cloud-white dome which, soaring, notes
The coming Morn and takes its first warm gleam
On the glad marble: — these, and joy of Life,

And ecstasy of Love, and youth and faith,
And marvels of the pictures painted us
By land and sea, and wonders in the lap
Which fold by fold the Mother opens us,
Whispering her secrets as we learn to hear —
And, at the last, that last large joy of all,
Trust in the goodness and the love of Him
Who, making so much well, will end all well:
These, as I think, are pages of Love's Book
Which here, with childhood's stammering lips, we spell;
And those who study deepest learn the most
That Love hates naught except Self-love — will have
Self-love uptorn, disdained, slain, cast away;
Will have us learn in Life's great book to be
Patient and reasonable, kindly and mild,
Led always by the hand of what we love
Nearer and nearer to the Loveliest,
The Largest, Highest, Fullest, Happiest, Best;

Despising none because 't is Allah made —
For shall men wrangle o'er the Nameless Name?—
And envying none because 't is Allah wills
What fortunes each shall have, and where his place:
But lief to live and not afraid to die,
Since Love, that would not wrong us, whispers oft
"Die now for me!" as though we could not die
Obeying Love! These are the echoes, Friends!
I catch from Sa'di and wise Hussein here;
Music for modern minds subtle — but yet
Sweet and contenting as those sounds which float
Around the snow-pure ceiling of yon tomb,
Lifting the heart on plumes of wings unseen,
And linking painful Earth with blissful Heaven.
Thus have I gathered — if I gather well.

MIRZA. Well hast thou gathered, Sir! and truly heard
The Sama', that deep murmur of the truth,
Which soundeth everywhere to ears unlocked:
And thereto lastly Sa'di leadeth us:

[*The* MIRZA *reads.*]

Was one God-loving — but he idly gave
His heart to be a cruel Beauty's slave:
Contempt he suffered; those that lately lauded
Beat Rumor's drum to call him fool and knave:

Yet all ill things he bore for her fair sake;
Love for Life's poison antidote doth make!
His neck to harsh rebuke he bowed; his forehead
Was bared for contumely to beat and break:

Nay — for all those reproachings were in vain;
Small heed hath one that drowns of pelting rain!
When Foot of Will strikes hard on Rock of Frenzy,
Who thinks of mud-splash, or of garment's stain?

And, one night, in the guise of her, Shaitân
Ensnared the heart of this bewildered man;

Soul-bound he lay in that delicious bondage,
And found no power of prayer when day began.

Angered against his flesh a pool he sought;
Winter upon the water's face had wrought
A marbled door of ice — he burst and plunged:
One cried: "Oh, Fool! to death thou wilt be brought!"

The youth said: "Vex me not with scorn and blame
If thus I punish Self. Five days the flame
Of Love had scorched my blood, consuming patience;
Now I extinguish it! for since I came

"Into this tender sin not once did she
Ask, with sweet throat, if ill or well I be;
Not once with gentle speech of grace and pity
Lighten the burden of Love's tyranny.

"But He! but He! Who made me from the clay,
And set my Soul within it, and alway

Pities and pardons, and enfolds us ever
In His beneficence, shall I not lay

"My heart back in His hand?" *Quoth Sa'di, too,*
Lose thyself thus if thou art lover true
Of Him where loss is gain! If otherwise,
Follow the path of flesh, and following, rue!

Yet, fear not, lost in God, dead earth to be;
He will remake, when He unmaketh thee!
There shoot no green blades from the wheat and barley
Till seed is laid in dust of husbandry.

That which doth set thee free from self shall bring
Nighness to God! This is a subtle thing
The selfless only know. Not self-possessing
Art thou thine own—but self-abandoning!

SAHEB. So are we back again on Christ's own Hill
In Syria; under the Tree with Buddh!

"Lose thyself," Sa'di says, "to find thyself";
The secret word of Love — but, will it come,
That hour which makes the sadness end in joy,
The worst turn best?

MIRZA. Surely that hour will come!
How else? The Master of the Cup keeps back
His richest vintage for last round of the Feast.
Is there not, Gulbadan! a song you sing,
Where some one asks the Pearl, the Rose, the Bird,
If it was hard to wait?

GULBADAN. *Chand wakt* — why, yes!
If it may please, I do remember that.

[GULBADAN *sings*.]

"How didst thou bear, white Pearl! the sea-waves' swelling,
The cold green underworld, where Day is Night?
The horrid monstrous fish, the dismal dwelling,
Shut in thy shell — such lustre lost to sight?"

"Oh, fair Princess! on whose neck I am gleaming,
I dreamed of thee — and now 't is no more dreaming!"

"How didst thou pass, red Rose! the bitter weather
While I was songless?" "Nightingale!" she said,
"I knew that Love and thou would come together!
In Bud of Patience Flower of Hope I laid
Till Zephyrs breathed, these blessèd moon-times bringing,
And now 't is summer, and I hear thee singing!"

"Why didst thou toil, bright Bird, thy soft nest weaving,
Early and late, hiding it in the tree;
The meadows and the pleasant sunshine leaving,
To build that little house?" "Oh, Poet! see
Under my wing five feathered chirping treasures!
Was I not wise to let go woodland pleasures?"

"How didst thou bring thy well-belovèd hither
Hand in hand, Lover with the happy eyes!
Not waiting till the Dead should rise together?
Knowest thou not that this is Paradise?"
"Angel of God! her step passed near my tomb
I heard it, and I rose, and I am come!"

SAHEB. I have a wish you too should dance for us
One last time, Dilazâr — as Nature does
Before Life's lesson closes, teaching men
What eyes were for, and hearts. There must have happed
Some last dance in this Garden for the Queen,
Some hour when all that love of Shah Jahan,
The stately days, the sovereignty, the bliss,
Gathered to golden finish like yon horn
Pointing the Taj. Dance and sing, Dilazâr!

[DILAZÂR *rises and dances slowly, accompanying her steps by the voice alone.*]

Eyes softly bold!
Bodice bound with gold!
Girdle clasping what love would enfold!
Light glancing feet
Which meet — part — and meet!
Dancing, dancing the measure sad and sweet:

Dance, dance still!
Dance, if you will,
All the night long as the slow stars dance!
All the night long
I would hear your Indian song,
And watch you, dark Star! in a trance.

Nay, 't is enough!
To the world rude and rough
Take back your heart, wistful Lover!
I have woven well the spell;
In your spirit it will dwell!
Remember me! the Dance and Song are over!

SAHEB. Even so, the changes and the charms of
Life
Dance to the heart and die away from eyes,
And Love takes off the bells, and we are left
To think, to sink, to die — at Burhanpur.
But that 's no end! the Sama' still is heard!

God's music cannot finish with one tune!
Hath Sa'di more upon this subtle theme?

MIRZA. Yet one piece more and then the end, good Friend!

[*The* MIRZA *reads.*]

Thus all around is Sama'—Music! they,
Who live in love of Heav'n ask none to play
Rabâb or pipe! the common sounds of Earth,
Make meanings! horse-hoofs clattering on the way,

Voices of waste and water, nay! a fly—
His gilded filmy wings he doth not ply
Before God's Lover, but that man puts, fly-like,
His hands across his head in ecstasy.

Full of those melodies of God heard here,
His Lover heeds not much for bam *or* zer,
High note or low note! To his eyes the call
Of wild birds winging home brings a glad tear:

For never anywhere one instant dumb
The Master of all Music doth become;
The great Chief-Singer sings — but what He sings
Sounds clear and dear only to ears of some.

Brothers! I say not what that Music is,
Nor when 't is heard aright, nor why the bliss
Of melody celestial sets life dancing,
Nor all the spell and mystery of this:

Needs that it find right hearer! If Soul's Bird
Launch wings from Tower of Truth at that Voice heard,
The Angels soar not higher: if a man
Be sunk in folly Shaitân speaks the word

Which holds him deaf. How should an evil ear
Catch the sweet whisper of the Sama' clear?
When midnight sitars play the loved one listens,
Not he whose senses steeped in wine-jars were.

When Zephyr breathes 't is the Rose nods to it,
Not that dead trunk which the steel axe must split!
The world is filled with Sama', with God speaking,
But harmony for deafness is unfit.

Say! hast thou marked the camel quicken speed,
And step forth joyous, when the Arab's reed
Pipes him a desert-strain? have camels gladness
At sweet sounds, and is man of baser breed?

SAHEB. Fain would we hear such strains, if we had grace!
But you who know all music, Gulbadan!
Is there still one of all your hundred songs
With echo of the Sama', of this sound
Unheard, yet sweeter than the things we hear?
GULBADAN. I unroll all my cloth of memory,
Searching for such, my Lord! If we please you,
We are well-pleased. Yes! there is this I know:
Dilazâr! play the "song without a sound."

[*She sings*, DILAZÂR *playing.*]

The Bulbul wailed, "Oh, Rose! all night I sing,
And Thou, Belovèd! utterest not one thing."
"Dear Bird!" she answered, "scent and blossoming
Are music of my Song without a sound."

The Cypress to the Tulip spake: "What bliss
Seest thou in sunshine, dancing still like this?"
"My cup," the Tulip said, "the wind's lips kiss;
Dancing I hear the Song without a sound."

The gray Owl hooted to the Dove at morn,
"Why art thou happy on thy jungle-thorn?"
"Hearest thou not," she cooed, "o'er Earth's face borne
This music of the Song without a sound?"

"Ah, Darweesh!" moaned a King, "Vainly I pray
For Allah's comfort, kneeling day by day."
"Sultan!" quoth he, "be meek, and hear alway
The music of His Mercy without sound."

"Poet!" a Queen sighed, "why alone to thee
Come visions of that world we cannot see —
Not great nor rich?" "I borrow minstrelsy,"
Smiling he said, "from Songs without a sound!"

Shirin-i-man! dear Lover! true and sweet,
Ask no more if I love, nor kiss my feet;
But hear, with cheek against my bosom's beat,
The music of the Song without a sound!

SAHEB. Fair ladies, thanks! the wind of morning lulls
Lest it lose half a note of your soft strain.
But here 's broad Day at last! we have outwatched
The Nightingales, and quite forgotten sleep.
How glorious comes the Morn! So it will come,
As I do hope, and as great Sa'di says,
After Life's night of loneliness and lack,
To all the Lovers who were tried and true.
So has it come, then — ages back — to him
That Sultan of the heart of Arjamand

Who loved his Queen so well, and laid her here:
Look, Gulbadan! — unless thy large black eyes
Be heavy with long vigil — how the Light
Walks like an Angel, making all things clear!
See, Dilazâr! the palm feathers are gilt
With new gold of another day for Earth,
And our Queen's tomb is turned to rose and pearl!
There must be some sweet Persian verse to praise
This perfect hour.

GULBADAN. We are not weary yet,
Since you are not; and we would serve you still
Who are not proud, and have such gentle thoughts
Not for the great ones only, but for us.
There comes a song to mind; Sister! play up
Chaman az nazim:

[*They sing alternate verses.*]

GULBADAN. The garden was laden with musk by the
breeze,

It whispered while Earth stirred, it rustled the
trees;
From the tresses of night fell the last loosened
star;
Ay! chaman az nazîm-i-sabah mushkbar!

DILAZÂR. The flowers ope'd their lids; from the wing
of the bird
The feathered head lifted; the jessamine heard
All pale in her charms as true Lovers' looks are,
Saman az latâfat chu rukhsar-i-yar!

GULBADAN. The Rose was awake ere the breath of
dawn blew,
With a tear on her cheek, as the Nightingale knew;
But she parted her lips now and lifted her face:
Zi bad-i-sahar gul dihan kurdah baz!

DILAZÂR. In the light of the morning her beautiful
breast
She bared for her lover, with passion confessed;

All smiling and nodding she gave him her grace;
Chu maâshuk-i-khandân aâshik nawâz![1]

MIRZA. Yea, Girl! thou canst not sing of love too sweet
So it be known that all these pretty words
Shadow the true words, play at baby joys,
Lisp the first letters of the larger life:
Yea, Girl! thou canst not drink this wine too deep,
Nor brim the cup too full, so it be known
The Cup-bearer is bliss, and not the wine,
The picture naught, the Painter all in all!
Sama'! Sama'! oh! hear, behind the strings,
Past voice of the Belovèd, past Morn's breath,
Past Rose and Nightingale, and yielded lips;
Past high delights of learning, lore and art,
Oh, beyond Sa'di even, God's sweet call

[1] These four *refrains* may be rendered literally:

"The garden was filled with musk by the breeze of morn."
"The jasmine, in delicacy, was as the cheek of the Beloved."
"The rose opened her lips to the breath of Dawn."
"Like a laughing beauty caressing her lover."

Lifting all hearts by *Jamâl* and *Jalâl*,
By Tenderness divine, and Majesty,
To Love and Life which have not place nor name!
Intoxicate yourselves with that wise dream,
Be Sûfi!

SAHEB. Must we don the woollen cap,
And drink in Shiah taverns?

MIRZA. Friend! the heart
Weareth no garb. But see! the Sun is come,
And hath his presence gloriously told,
Like a great King before whose feet they spread
The crimson carpet of expectancy!
Now must we part, belated Birds of night,
Who talked, i' the dark, of Love and Life some while,
Yet blink, only to look at this gold hem
Of Heaven's hid splendor which men call the Morn.
You will not quite forget the Ishk, and us,
The roses we outwatched, the nightingales
That vexed their hearts, and stayed their burning songs,

And gathered round, for enviousness to hear
Gulbadan's voice, and strings of Dilazâr?

SAHEB. Never shall I forget!

MIRZA. And when men say,
In your 'Wilâyeti' beyond the seas,
That Islam hath no deep philosophics,
Will you not speak of Sa'di and the night
We sate together underneath this Taj;
And tell your people? Dilazâr! read yet
Ba dil goftam az Misr to the Saheb:

[DILAZÂR *reads.*]

In many lands I have wandered, and wondered, and listened and seen;
And many my friends and companions and teachers and lovers have been.

And nowhere a corner was there but I gathered up pleasure and gain,
From a hundred gardens rose-blooms, from a thousand granaries grain;

And I said to my Soul in secret "Oh, thou who from
journeys art come!
It is meet we should bear some token of love to the
stayers at home;

For where is the traveller brings not from Nile the
sweet green reed,
Or Kashmiri silk, or musk-bags, or coral, or cardamom-
seed?"

I was loath from all that Pleasaunce of the Sun, and
its words and ways,
To come to my country giftless, and showing no fruit
of my days:

But if my hands were empty of honey, and pearls and
gold,
There were treasures far sweeter than honey, and
marvellous things to be told,

Whiter than pearls, and brighter than the cups at a
Sultan's feast,
And these I have brought for love-tokens, from the
Lords of Truth, in my East.

SAHEB. Yes! for I know a Friend who is as I
Your lover, and a seeker for the Truth,
And he will strive to teach what Sa'di taught
Among my people, if this Persian Rose
Under our skies can open her rich leaves,
And western Nightingales sing praise to them!
Mirza! my grateful hand! Angels of God
Say some day to your gentle soul in Heaven,
Khûsh Âmadid![1] Dilazâr! tie this gold
Tight in your cloth, and keep one Saheb's name
Green in your thoughts, as our Queen's Garden
is!
And Gulbadan! dear Gulbadan! I kiss
That little palm which took the baby safe
Forth from the tiger's jaws; I praise and press
These gentle lips which sang so meltingly:
To-morrow I will send your wounded arm,
Which bears its red hurt like a Rose of God,

1 "You are welcome!"

The golden armlet! Ah! not thanks! I owe
More than much gold — more than you know — to
you.
Remember me!

GULBADAN. *Inshallah!* till we die!

Cambridge: John Wilson & Son, University Press.